P9-DWT-232

# iLead

## Five Insights for Building Sustainable Organizations

Blooming Twig Books / New York

# What readers are saying about iLead:

*"iLead is a book for leadership in our fast paced modern time. It provides practical ideas for leaders and motivational techniques, not just in business, but in all its forms – even political organizations."*

- **Hon. Wayne Easter, PC MP**, Former Solicitor General of Canada

*"It's one thing to write a book about leadership concepts. It's quite another thing for the author to have actually done and lived what's written about. That's the real value of this book and you'll sense that from the first page on."*

- **Ian Percy**, Author of *Going Deep: Exploring Spirituality in Life and Leadership*

*"Joe Sherren brings to the table a solid management background, combined with an in-depth knowledge of leadership and management theory. This enables him to separate the wheat from the chaff and present theory in terms that are easy to understand, painless to implement and proven (first hand) to work."*

- **Allan M. Stewart**, President, Human Synergistics Canada

*"Joe Sherren has provided a business model to allow business leaders to do business better, and his approach emphasizes the need for today's management to work to learn before working to earn."*

- **Michael Cassidy**, President of the Cassidy Group of Companies
Assistant Professor University of Prince Edward Island

*"iLead hits the nail right on the head. Joe's insights and ideas will be the road map of how future industries and companies will lead and succeed. This book changed my business philosophy."*

- **Bill Tkach**, Vice President of Sales, Heritage Education Funds Inc.

# iLead
**Five Insights for Building Sustainable Organizations**
Copyright © 2011 Joseph Sherren
*www.ilead.ca*

Published by
Blooming Twig Books
PO Box 4668 #66675
New York, NY 10163-4668
*www.bloomingtwig.com*

**ISBN 978-1-933918-68-6**

First Edition, First Printing

**Dedicated to my grandchildren, Mikayla and Garret.**
It is my dream that when they begin their careers,
they (and everyone else's grandchildren)
will enjoy a healthy workplace
with constructive iLeaders.

# iLead

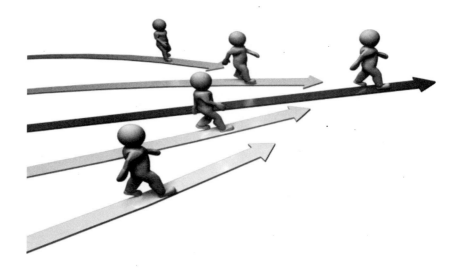

## Joseph Sherren

Blooming Twig Books / New York

# Table of Contents

# Foreword

*by Howard Putnam*
Former CEO of Southwest Airlines & Braniff International Airways
International Speaker and Author of *The Winds of Turbulence*

I grew up on a farm in Iowa, with positive reinforcement all around me. Although we had no electricity until I was ten years old, my parents and two older siblings lit the spark within me that later enabled me to be an effective leader and CEO.

Looking back, I see my father as an iLeader who was inspiring and passionate about three F's: family, farming and flying. We had a small 200-acre farm where we raised registered Hereford cattle along with corn, oats, alfalfa and more. Family was always very important to him, and my father fostered a culture within all of us that focused on attitudes and harnessed our collective energies. My father convinced my mother that if he sold enough calves and pigs to raise $600, he could buy a used airplane, a J-3 Piper Cub. He had held a vision for years that he would someday fly, own and keep an airplane. He did just that, and he taught me to fly in my early teens.

After my father, I had the opportunity to work with some great iLeaders in my career. One of them was Eddie Carlson, the Chairman and CEO of United Airlines, when I was a young Vice President of Marketing there. Looking back, he was the epitome of Joe Sherren's *Five Insights*.

1. He laid a strong foundation to grow and prosper in both good times and in crisis.

2. He was a people person, a motivator and led by example.

3. He coached and mentored without realizing the impact he was having on me and others who went on to positions of greater responsibility.

4. He communicated brilliantly with all employees and stakeholders – something amazing to watch.

5. He defined our culture by saying, "No one sings solo," helping us instead to succeed as a team.

Later in my career, as the second CEO of Southwest Airlines and then as the CEO of Braniff International, all of Joe's *Five Insights* came into play for me personally.

At Southwest Airlines, we defined the people culture by saying: "Always hire *attitudes* and develop *skills*." iLead is written in a down to earth and understandable manner, and if you have the passion and ambition to take your leadership role to new heights here are "Five Insights for Building Sustainable Organizations," no matter how small or how large they are.

Joe Sherren has laid out a great flight plan for current times, and well into the future. You need to read this before you take off.

# Preface

All great leaders were at one time not-very-good managers. Fortunately, management is a skill that everyone can learn, especially if they have the desire and are willing to put in the time and effort to learn.

My life in business began when my dad (at the age of 68) began another profession. He purchased a small grocery store. He then promptly experienced cardiac issues, which meant I ended up, at the age of 15, running the business. I was responsible for ordering, stocking, pricing, sales, hiring, firing and just overall managing the operations of the business. I did this while attending high school full time.

My next experience in business came from working with a very brilliant entrepreneur, Hollis Corney, who owned a group of clothing stores. He was not highly educated, but one of the smartest business people I have ever worked with. It started out as a summer job, and then developed into a partnership of selling clothing and shoes from the back of a pickup truck. I travelled the province cold calling and selling dry goods to farms, small businesses and students from that truck. Some of the greatest lessons in making a business profitable while treating all people with compassion and fairness I still use today came from working with Hollis many years ago.

After that I joined a Fortune 500 company where I had an amazing career and developed a passion for learning. After enjoying much success in various positions, I was promoted to management. Again, I figured they promoted me because I worked harder, felt that I was smarter, knew more, and understood the business better than those around me. I figured that everyone should listen to me and do what I say.

My first year as a manager was one of the toughest years of my life. After about 18 months I found myself working hard, staying late while all my staff members were going home on time. I was spending nights and weekends at the office; they were at home enjoying their families. I became discouraged and often wondered, *Why do I even want to be a manager?* Even some of my staff members were earning more money than I was. Eventually I burned myself out.

It took a while, but then I smartened up. I was also fortunate that my company was willing to invest in my development as a manager. I spent time educating myself, spending time with mentors, and learning the psychology of management. I also first heard an expression I've used ever since: "People don't care how much you know until they know how much you care."

At that time, I wholeheartedly began to put my employees' interests and needs before my own. I learned that I personally could not motivate people because people need to be intrinsically motivated. What a manager has to do is provide the environment, opportunity and support for employees to achieve their own personal goals while working on company objectives.

I was very fortunate to work for a company that was values-driven, and truly understood how important it was to respect every individual within the organization, no matter what position. The company also believed that if you honor colleagues and employees, they would honor you back. If you look after *people*, they will look after the *business*. Investing in people will in fact provide the best return for your money.

This enabled me to get another chance and go on to win management awards at various levels and enjoy many successes. This was also the foundation that gave me the passion and training to help other managers by providing them with the secrets to: managing more people, working less hard, achieving higher employee morale and ultimately being less stressed.

While putting this book together, I interviewed a number of very successful leaders. In this book, I refer to leaders who sincerely want to achieve higher productivity and make their employees happier as *iLeaders*. I have profiled one iLeader at the end of each chapter. Although these featured leaders have achieved their success in different industries, they all share a number of similarities. This book is a summary of some of those concepts.

My sincere hope is that that there will be a time when all employees are able to enjoy a healthy workplace with constructive managers. This is my humble contribution towards that goal.

*- Joe Sherren, June 2011*

# Introduction

## A Case for iLeadership

*"The future is not what it used to be."*
- Yogi Berra

Over the next decades we will see more transition in the workplace than ever before. We will certainly soon look back on our current technology the same way we now look at Victrolas, black and white television sets and rotary telephones.

As Mark Twain said: "I'm all for progress. It is change I object to." Our ability to overcome the initial apprehension we have to the challenges of new technology and business practices will be crucial to our survival in the marketplace.

The challenges of the coming years require a new and more malleable brand of leader. I call this leader an *iLeader* (insightful Leader), which I define as a leader with the ability to manage more people, increase productivity, and be less stressed. An iLeader stands with eyes wide open and looks into the future with the most powerful telescope available.

An especially forward-looking study conducted by the Conference Board of Canada[1] is an appropriate introduction to the concept of iLeadership. The study pointed out ten major changes iLeaders should be aware of in order to stay ahead of the curve in these changing times.

### 1. Boomers are back & Millennials are coming.

Across North America, the integration of four generations is already happening. The first wave of Baby Boomers who were born in the late 1940s and 1950s are returning to the workplace for several reasons. Economic difficulties in every sector, and changes in governmental regulations are making retirement less attractive. At the same time, Gen X and the Millennials are now sharing duties, workspaces, ideas, incomes and job titles.

### 2. White guys will be minorities too.

In North America, a falling domestic birth rate and rising immigration are leading to a day when the majority of urban workers will not be middle-aged white guys. This trend of increasing diversity is already close to reality in many large cities, and will over time allow for a constant flow of new products and services, opening new conduits to global markets.

However, many challenges will accompany the positive change that increased diversity and global business will bring in coming years. How will the workplace effectively represent the needs of all minorities? And perhaps more importantly, how will corporations increasingly and

---

[1] *Navigating Through the Storm: Leaders and the World of Work in 2020.*
*See: http://www.conferenceboard.ca/documents.aspx?did=3541, last accessed 6/2011.*

successfully integrate minorities into the senior levels of corporate management?

### 3. We will all be linked to work 24/7.

A decade ago, BlackBerry® Smartphones were just starting to tether us to work. A select few others used Treos and Palm Pilots as daily planners and sometimes telephones. Now, iPods, iPads, iPhones and "iLearning" are the way of the world.

In similar fashion, imagine how completely technology will connect us in the year 2020. Envision the tall fences we will need to erect in order to ensure that work will not encroach upon our privacy and leisure time. "Personal life" as a concept we have known our entire lives is in for a major overhaul.

### 4. It will be back to the future.

Remember the good old days when we made almost everything we consumed with our own two hands? Well, those days are coming back.

In today's technologically advanced social climate, individuals are now able to publish their own books, create their own software, games, music albums and just about anything else imaginable. This creation and production of products that they will consume themselves (the new word for this is "prosumerism") will spur producers to make their products consumer-friendly like never before. There is already a resurgence of community-based consumerism where a customer deals with people they know and trust, and these social systems will continue to grow in the near and distant future.

### 5. Employees will not be prisoners of corporate cages.

Advances in technology will result in ever-increasing connectivity that will enable productive work from a distance, whether in our backyards, at a coffee shop, on the beach or on a flight to Arizona. The old factorial model that says, "You are my prisoner from nine to five," will slowly die away.

Instead of usual office meetings, workers will connect on Facebook, Twitter, LinkedIn and other social media inventions of the coming years, allowing groups of workers to collaborate on projects in new and intuitive ways.

### 6. Wi-Fi & intellectual capital replace bricks & mortar.

Many corporations today already have an online existence that is as well known as their presence in the streets. A decade from now, virtual locations will most likely outnumber physical locations, and the entire system will shift. The iLeader must be ready for this. People will be paid for what they know and can deliver, not for their time. This will require corporations who attempt to thrive in the new environment to rethink everything. Banks and lending institutions must then also rethink their methods and policies for assessing worth, solvency and potential.

### 7. Top-down leadership cultures will disappear.

Flexible work schedules, workplaces and management systems will create highly decentralized workforces.

If most of the workers are out of the office, sharing jobs or working online, it will be hard for even the best of management to remain in "command and control". iLeaders must step in and create a new process of decision-making within the corporation.

### 8. Independent contractors will become the norm.

More part-time, seasonal and contract workers will help companies adjust in advance to quick changes in the type and amount of work that needs to be done. However, virtual and part-time workers are usually less loyal to the business entity and make it harder to enforce a single corporate culture. The iLeader will rethink what corporate culture entails, and how to empower workers to effectively integrate into the team.

### 9. Teamwork will be a mandatory skill.

For years now, many organizations have simply *played* with the idea of creating a team dynamic in the workplace. Within these companies, there is little *true* commitment, and the team continues to run on its top-down hierarchal engine. In the future, a new kind of teamwork will be required.

iLeaders must work hard to implement a functional system that can sustain the team into the unforeseeable future.

### 10. Social networking will become the teams of tomorrow.

In the future, within a multigenerational and multicultural workplace, pursuit of true teamwork will be mandatory. However, teams will be virtual. Problems will be more complex so iLeaders will capitalize on the concept of mass collaboration and value employees with the ability to work in the new team settings.

*"The world hates change, yet it is the only
thing that has brought progress."*
- Charles Kettering

## The Five Insights

With the right combination of awareness and skills, the workplace of the future will carry amazing opportunity.

I have encountered a myriad of leaders at various stages of their careers in my years of training and speaking to organizations. I break down all of these iLeaders' management styles and characteristics into the following Five Insights.

## The First Insight

iLeaders understand how organizations naturally evolve. They are aware that crises will occur at each phase of transformation in their organization's development. Leaders will then be prepared for each crisis as it arrives, and be able to proactively address and minimize its negative impact on customers and employees.

I compare this in my speeches to the responsibilities of an airline pilot. At the beginning of a given flight, pilots predict that there might be turbulence. In order to prevent injury to their passengers or crew, the pilots ask them to buckle their seat belts so they are prepared for turbulence – just in case.

In order for organizations to grow and evolve even during times of smooth sailing, they must buckle their metaphorical seat belts and modify their thinking, behaviors, culture and leadership. iLeaders create and implement long-term strategies for success despite the turbulence that may lie ahead.

## The Second Insight

One of the greatest challenges for an iLeader is attracting the right employees and providing an environment whereby those employees become intrinsically motivated. An iLeader achieves this in a number of ways. For example, an effective talent management process can help to greatly reduce turnover and services while increasing overall employee morale.

The "behavioral interviewing" system is one of the strongest methods of managing talent. Behavioral interviewing can be used during the hiring process and involves asking open-ended questions to determine a prospective employee's thinking patterns and problem-solving processes. Once a viable applicant has been pinpointed by the behavioral interview, their resume will fill in the background necessary for proper hiring.

Once the right people are hired, the iLeader also creates an environment that motivates people to stay. They do this by truly understanding the diversity of workers and ensuring that there is a workplace that supports true collaboration and a management structure that provides a place that harnesses the true potential of all the workers.

Doing this requires a unique understanding of effective coaching and how individuals are motivated differently. Each person's motivation will change as they grow and develop in their profession.

## The Third Insight

An iLeader promotes the right people into management and then ensures that they receive effective training and development. This will ensure team success.

I have heard certain executives say, "You are either born to be a leader or not." That is cow-paddy! Everyone has the potential to be a great leader. Training iLeaders to be coaches will make all the difference.

Effective coaches give advice and counsel to their clients as well as providing them emotional support. iLeaders should do the same with their employees, asking powerful questions that lead to solutions within the organization as well as within each individual.

There are a number of models of teaching iLeaders to be coaches. Some of them are good, and others not so good. But what is important is that, regardless of the method, iLeaders have a simple-to-understand concept, and easy-to-implement process with which they are comfortable.

The success of iLeaders' coaching is of course largely dependent on their ability to connect with and communicate in a way that is most appropriate for each employee. People (genetically) communicate certain ways from birth. Knowing this helps iLeaders adapt their messages in a way that is received more positively. Doing this will ensure a higher level of trust and understanding.

*Throughout this book, I will be detailing the following five-step process to figure out and stick with a plan of action:*

1. ***Know the Trends.***
   Managers at every level have to be ready for what is coming.

2. ***Clarify the Implications.***
   Figure out what all this change will mean for your company or workplace.

3. ***Identify Needs and Opportunities.***
   Once you know the organizational changes that need to take place, create the strategies that will proactively address those changes and not just react to them.

4. ***Create Strategies to Address Change.***
   Your management team must now have, or should be developing the skills to capitalize on the trends that are happening.

5. ***Be Prepared.***
   Remember, it wasn't raining when Noah decided to build the ark. In my seminars, I do not focus on teaching people what to do, but rather on how to think. If we can teach people how to think - they will figure out what to do.

## The Fourth Insight

iLeaders foster an environment where all members of their organizations are able to engage in constructive communication. Because each individual has a genetic predisposition for one of twelve communication styles, iLeaders can adapt their communication accordingly. These are not "personality styles". They are models that help iLeaders reach a more holistic view of any individual (and themselves) and determine how best to relate.

One model I will present looks at genetic make-up and predetermines communication preferences. Another looks at how people have been conditioned to think based on past experiences. Still another looks at behavior and determines how this can lead to success or failure when working with others. And in the coaching section I will show how people respond based on their competency to perform a specific task.

## The Fifth Insight

iLeaders work hard to create a collaborative culture within their organizations, and with increasing generational and global diversity in the workplace, this fifth insight is the most important.

Every successful organization must create a culture of collaboration where employees have control over *how* they do their work in order to survive. The most effective teams will have workers who come to work enthusiastically motivated. Each should have one thing in mind when they arrive at work: "How can I make someone else in the organization look better today?"

Creating such an environment harnesses the collective potential of all individuals in the organization and helps to create a powerful team dynamic. The company thus protects and insures itself against damage from competing organizations and other challenges.

For years I always felt better working 16 hours a day for myself than eight hours working for someone else. Many of the current executives with whom I have spoken shared a similar perspective in their younger years. However, when they eventually landed a job with a corporation that did give them the kind of latitude they desired, where they felt like they worked for themselves, they described a stronger sense of loyalty as well as increased productivity and happiness in the workplace.

I have great admiration for the six executives I interviewed for the iLeader Profiles in this book, and the countless others with whom I have conversed over the last decades. I have included a summary of one insightful interview at the end of each chapter.

# iLeader Profile

## *Dr. Christopher Mazza*

*Dr. Christopher Mazza is the President, Chief Executive Officer, and driving force behind the creation of Ornge. Under his leadership, Ontario's aero medical transport program has been transformed from a disparate series of air ambulance programs into an organization with a clear mission, vision, and values. Dr. Mazza's combined expertise in the fields of health care and business has been a key component of Ornge's success thus far.*

When I spoke with Dr. Christopher Mazza I asked him how he was able to achieve as much as he has in such a short period of time. He told me one word: "Passion". This is what differentiates him from the normal corporate leader, gives him the drive to pursue everything he dreams of, and drives him to continue even when at the point of exhaustion. Passion for his work, passion for the wellbeing of all of his clients, passion for his family, passion for the people who work for him, and passion for life.

Dr. Mazza's desire is to leave a legacy. Not with just a few patients whom his ideas have saved, but, with the over 13 million potential human beings who will live to see another day because he achieved his vision. And he sees possibilities that others cannot. His personal mission is to always impact lives positively. He does not wait for the sick and injured to come to a hospital; he brings healing to the place it is needed in a timely and effective manner.

After his humble beginnings on a farm, Dr. Mazza spent 11 years in medical training, which includes over six years in the Emergency Department of a hospital where he continues to practice. In this role, he learned quickly that management plays just as significant a role in success as does skill in medicine. In that environment, efficient and well-managed systems combined with clear-thinking managers make the difference between life and death.

Dr. Mazza breaks down any great management system into the following seven strategic areas:

1. **Discovery**
2. **Strategy**
3. **Vision**
4. **People**
5. **Execution**
6. **Organization**
7. **Metrics**

Dr. Mazza feels that the reason for a breakdown in communications between the leaders and the frontline staff in an organization is that leaders have to continually think of and live in the future, but the staff must operate in the present. Therefore, it is critical that middle managers ensure that communication is flowing freely in both directions.

Dr. Mazza says a key ingredient to the long-term success and growth of an organization is to consciously focus on developing a constructive culture. In Ornge, the three values that guide the organization, its vision and all decisions are: compassion, collaboration and innovation.

iLeaders must also be committed to following their own strategy and vision to execution with talented people on their teams. Within his own organization to this day, what gives Dr. Mazza the most pleasure is to watch team members grow, develop, and achieve success.

*Dr. Mazza is an Ivey Scholar for Scholastic Excellence in the Masters of Business Administration Program at the University of Western Ontario. He is also an Associate Professor at the University of Toronto Faculty of Medicine, and is frequently called upon to advise governments on a variety of matters related to transport medicine, emergency medicine, critical care surge capacity, and pandemic planning.*

Whether you are a six-figure executive or an entry-level manager, you will achieve great things if you adopt and employ the principles of the iLeader. This book is designed to complement your natural potential and provide you with knowledge and skill-building in order to bring and polish those intrinsic abilities, just as polishing a stone brings out its intrinsic yet hidden natural beauty.

# Summary

## *Introduction*

### The workplace is changing.

- *The Millennials are coming.*
- *Baby Boomers are coming back.*
- *Social networks will be the communities of the future.*

### Employees will escape corporate cages.

- *Top-down bureaucratic cultures will disappear.*
- *Independent Contractors will be the norm.*

### The *Five Insights* for successful leaders.

1. *Insightful leaders know how organizations evolve.*
2. *Insightful leaders are effective coaches.*
3. *Insightful leaders hire and retain the right people.*
4. *Insightful leaders engage in constructive communication.*
5. *Insightful leaders create collaborative cultures.*

# Chapter One

## *Growing the Business*

*"Conformity is the jailer of freedom and the enemy of growth."*
- John F. Kennedy

E very decade brings business challenges and economic downturns. Fortunately, a solution always comes along and life goes on. In the end, there are companies who are winners and there are others who do not survive. So the real question is: Why — in the same business climate, with similar quality products, similar quality employees, and in similar markets — do some companies not only survive but thrive during the turbulence, while others are left behind?

iLeaders whose companies do well in spite of economic downturns and an uncertain future have three things in common:

1. They understand there is a predictable pattern to growth and are able to evolve their culture, leadership, and personal development programs to be most effective.

2. They create, set, document, and track their progress against a set of clearly articulated goals that will determine where they want to be one, five, ten, and twenty years from now.

3. They understand the changing needs of the workforce and are able to discard outdated traditions, policies, and processes. They adapt their culture to one that will harness the collective potential of each employee.

This chapter teaches the iLeader how to navigate the inevitable turbulence that will eventually come.

## Distinct and Predictable Growth Phases

Most organizations are formed because a group of people share a dream about a product they want to bring to market, a service they want to provide a community, or a dream to make the world a better place to live. When they come together to implement that dream, they work in a very unique organizational culture that is necessary for survival.

As organizations evolve through their various phases of development, they also experience a distinct crisis each time they transition to the next stage. I will review here the phases and some of the crises that must be overcome in order to ensure survival.

## 1. Entrepreneurial Phase

During this phase, everyone shares a common dream and works together. There are no limitations of policy manuals and organization charts. The workplace is fun and lively, but profits are minimal since the focus and financial measurements are on revenue growth and market penetration. Employees are truly inspired and intrinsically motivated. They can see the bigger picture and how they each fit into achieving the ultimate goal.

Employees communicate with each other on a regular basis, often in the form of team huddles rather than mandatory meetings with strict agendas. Individuals are able to make decisions unencumbered by autocratic systems and a bureaucratic chain of command. For instance, the shipping room clerk may be struggling with one of his work challenges. If the president walks by, the two people might engage in a discussion on how the packages should be bundled. Or, in another part of the firm, a salesperson might go to the boss and say, "I think I have a prospect out in Vancouver." The boss might reply, "Good luck. Do you need some cash or a credit card? You know what is best... Do whatever it takes."

This is an exciting time in a company's growth, and it requires a set of unique individuals working independently, with high trust, towards common goals. There is no need for a policy manual because everyone knows the expected code of behavior and the reputation required to be successful in that particular industry. Although the company is a fun place to work, everyone works very hard and adds value on a daily basis. In this phase, the most important measures are market share and revenue growth, both driving value and stock prices.

Over the long term, if a company *continues* working in this manner, it will be following a *going-out-of-business* strategy. My studies show that nearly 70% of entrepreneurial companies do not survive past a ten-year period.

The organizations that do succeed realize they must institute measured controls and processes to continue to grow. They begin to understand the danger of unilateral decision-making by managers and staff. Employees must also learn to work smarter, not harder. This realization causes the iLeader to start documenting many rules, processes and systems. This will naturally guide the company into the next phase.

## 2. Bureaucratic Phase

Companies must develop systems and processes that have checks and balances in order to remain viable. Some are able to make it into the bureaucratic phase on their own, and others end up merging with or being bought out by larger organizations that stimulates a faster evolution.

In the Bureaucratic Phase, iLeaders establish the necessary policy manuals, organization charts, and reporting mechanisms without assembling unwieldy and largely ineffective autocratic structures.

The main driver in this phase is often profit, and while the bottom line grows more important, decisions are made that result in cuts to customer service and staff development. As a result, a high level of uncertainty will emerge, leading to dissatisfied employees with a high level of stress in the workplace.

For optimal success, iLeaders in this phase should follow the 8 x 5 rule. This means that those who hold the title of manager must have at least eight people reporting to them. Also, there should be no more than five levels of reporting structure.

I have seen many organizations in the past create as many as 15 levels of management, with 15 layers of bureaucracy between the executives and the customer, who brings (green) dollars into the organization.

So many organizations in this phase spend more time passing (brown) dollars between departments, creating what appears to be movement by actually calling other departments and units "customers". But really, this is just wheel-spinning and does nothing to advance the organization towards its ultimate purpose. Informal studies show that around 50% of organizations that get stuck in this phase fail to make it past 20 years.

When organizations in this phase reach their peak, crisis management takes over. Their solution is often to downsize, right-size, and restructure. Unfortunately, this leaves a bad taste for even the employees who remain with the organization. I call them the walking wounded. iLeaders instead lead a battle cry during this phase: "Get closer to the customer." They work to create strategic specific business units (SBUs), divisions, functions, and lines of business (LoBs). These units are then aligned with their specific product or service offerings. This will now result in the company evolving into its next phase of development.

## 3. Silo Phase

A "silo" is an organizational structure in which units are created to focus on specific products or services. During the silo phase, companies are organized into Lines of Business (LOB's), Strategic Business Units (SBU's), Functions, or Divisions.

Elliott Jacques details the benefits of this phase in his book *Requisite Organization*. Although the organization, by reaching this phase, will have fixed many of the issues encountered during the bureaucratic phase, new problems will now emerge.

One possible problem is that the silos often do not communicate with each other. This lack of communication causes employee frustration and duplication of effort.

### *During the Silo Phase,*
### *Managers behave like a herd of fighting bulls.*

Employees may also scatter their energies in this phase, chasing ideas designed only for short-term gain. These efforts may divert them from the company's core business strengths, often with disastrous results.

In addition, the heads of each of these silos could become engaged in what is known as "empire building," with each unit vying for its own human resources department, research and development function, and salesforce. Departments and business units fight against each other for limited, budgeted resources and the attention of the senior management. This frequently leads to duplication of effort and additional costs not supported by higher revenues.

During this period, customers are called on from several salespeople all from the same organization, representing the various units seeking their business. When customers call the company, their calls often go to an outsourced call center where they might even be treated rudely by the staff. An all-too-commonly phrase heard is: "Not my job." Customers become confused and frustrated, since the purchasing process is a time-consuming and expensive one.

In such a situation, customers leave in search of a company that cares more about them. In this age of customer service, clients demand quality, service, customization, convenience, speed, and personal contact.

iLeaders think of their customers' needs first and push for evolution that supports that goal. They fix the customer service problems, and work to change the silos to be more customer-driven. Instead of being focused on the company's specific products or services, the silos are re-aligned and the battle cry becomes: "Market-Driven Management!"

### 4. Matrix Phase

In the Matrix Phase, the silos still exist, but the focus shifts from products or services to the customer's industry, size or geographic coverage. Consequently, there is only one human resources manager across all divisions, one research & development manager, and one account manager.

|  | Unit 1 | Unit 2 | Unit 3 |
|---|---|---|---|
| Dept. |  |  |  |
| Dept. |  |  |  |
| Dept. |  |  |  |

The Matrix Phase brings its share of new problems to the forefront. The most significant of these is an exponential increase in the number of "meetings."

These meetings were implemented in order to avoid the disenfranchisement of employees. But if everyone gives input on every little decision, productivity drops. In this phase, there is lots of motion but no movement. If you were to walk into this corporation, you would see everyone running around with little day timers, or iPads, under their arms, heading to another meeting. If you talk to an employee and ask, "What did you do today?" they will say, "Meetings, bloody meetings." When you ask, "What are you doing tomorrow?" They respond, "I have a meeting at 9:00, a meeting at lunch, another at 1:30." If you ask, "When are you going to go talk to a customer?" they will say, "I don't have time; I am in too many meetings."

Another problem that emerges is that no one knows to whom they "report". When you ask, "Who do you work for?" an employee's response is often confused or ambivalent. They say things like, dotted line to him, and dotted line to her. This sort of structure results in a lack of consistency.

Some companies have even gone so far as to come up with new names for meetings in order to disguise them. They call them *networking sessions, interlocking events, cross-functional synergy sessions,* or *dialogue opportunities.* Other organizations even have meetings just to decide when and where to have *future* meetings. Under any name, they are still meetings, and employees come to hate them.

Conversely, in the Matrix Phase, iLeaders are customer-focused suppliers. This means that they work to empower the front-line staff, who can truly make a difference to a customer (who are really what I call Vice Presidents of First Impressions) must be educated appropriately in the values, vision, mission, and critical objectives of the company, of which have been created through an all-inclusive collaborative strategic planning process.

Strategic planning starts with the executive team. But then it cascades to all managers, then all supervisors, then all employees. Every employee should have an opportunity to provide input or comment before anything is cast in stone.

At this point, iLeaders begin to ask, "Is there a better way?" They seek out an efficient bureaucracy, with silos focused on customers, and cross-functional synergies that work across the organization instead of in separate silos.

## 5. Empowerment Phase

I have a big caution here. Some organizations that decide to move into the Empowerment Phase either try to go through the process on their own with an internal facilitator, or hire someone who does not have the depth and experience required to help usher in this cultural transformation. Many take reductionist academic approaches that often leave out important steps. Such methods often lead to nothing more than fancy slogans under inspirational posters on the wall or motivational marketing statements in the organization's Annual Report.

Many companies hire a consultant who takes the executives to a nice resort for some visioning and strategic planning. There's nothing wrong with that. But some of these consultants must have been paid by the word, because some of these Vision statements and Mission statements come back with phrases like, "We are going to be the best in customer service and excel at everything we do, with happy and productive people, and we will do in a timely fashion, and with suppliers who are partners, and *blah blah blah.*"

Some of these consultants must also have relatives in the picture framing business, because the statements are always introduced to the employees in large, beautiful glass frames. Then all the staff are all brought into the cafeteria for a Monday morning meeting where they are presented with a "wonderful" product. Consequently management wonders why the employees were not totally excited about the whole event or mission statement.

At this point, iLeaders think, "Wouldn't it be great if everyone could just have that spirit and commitment they had during the entrepreneurial phase?" Well, some successfully explored that possibility. Their objective was to create that culture but in a large existing organization. The phrase "*intra*-preneurial organization" was then coined.

These companies dissected the elements that could make an entrepreneurial culture work in their current environment. One of the basic elements that came out was *values*. During the Entrepreneurial Phase, this was the foundation people used to make their decisions. For example, they knew their reputation was the most important aspect of long-term success and so they placed great emphasis on it.

Another element was for all the people in the firm to share the same *dream*. However, in the 1990s, since it was not cool for executives to talk about *dreaming*, they used the word *vision* instead. In its simplest form, the vision of a company *is* the dream for which the corporation is striving. It is the guiding light on the other side of the ocean, which the organization ultimately hopes to reach.

During those early entrepreneurial days, everyone knew why they came to work, and the consequences of accomplishing (or not) what they had to do. This knowledge became their mission—the reason they came to work on a day-to-day basis. Each organization should be able to answer one fundamental question: What is the reason for your organization's existence today? The one-sentence answer to this is the organization's mission statement.

Out of this values-vision-mission framework, iLeaders then create their strategic objectives. These objectives are annual goals that should focus on three key areas to ensure success for the organization. The critical areas are as follows:

1. **Business requirements** This area is measured by such items as revenue growth, profit, market-share, return on investment, return on assets, earnings before income tax, depreciation and amortization, and return on total assets. Most organizations are good at planning and tracking these on a monthly, quarterly, or annual basis.

2. **Customer satisfaction** This important area is measured by "client" loyalty, "referrals", repeat business, satisfaction surveys, and complaint letters. My studies show that less than 50% of organizations are taking a

proactive approach and tracking these with a strategy for improvement on a regular basis.

3. **Employee morale** This area is also measured in terms of loyalty. The matrix phase looks at attrition, punctuality, absenteeism, morale assessment surveys, and executive interviews. Would you believe that less than 25% of North American organizations have a year-end target, a strategy to help them achieve it, and a measurement system to monitor progress?

iLeaders are able to keep these three fundamental areas in balance. If one does very well to the detriment of the others, it will ultimately damage the organization. By focusing on these three key areas, the primary measurement in the next phase becomes the "balanced scorecard".

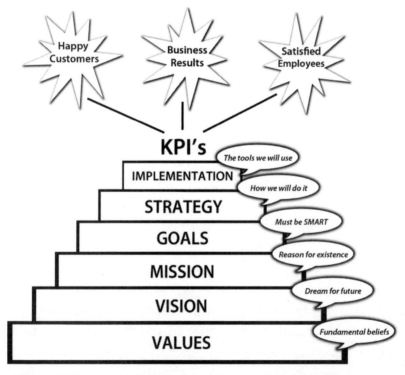

## The Formal Planning Process

## 6. Empowered Teams

When an organization completes the whole process, it is then able to go on to the next phase, which is the culture of *empowerment*. This is when all employees, managers, associates and union members connect. They connect because they have now all bought into, will benefit from, and are committed to the organization's strategic plan. In the following pages I will review the critical elements of effective strategic planning.

However, in the Empowered Team phase, staff members are guided by the plan and the foundation of all activities and decisions are based on that plan. In this phase, the measurement becomes the balanced scorecard. The three elements of the scorecard are:

1. Business Results
2. Customer Satisfaction and
3. Employee Morale

*"Purpose is the most powerful motivator in the world."*
- Mahatma Gandhi

## Live The Vision

A study done by *Psychology Today* magazine indicated that more than 90 percent of workers surveyed said they want to produce the highest-quality work possible. In that same survey, however, more than 50 percent said they only work hard enough to keep their jobs. The reason they gave was that they were frustrated with management practices and archaic policies.

In order to tap into true employee enthusiasm, iLeaders tear down the top-down policies and authority-based cultures, and give people work and "the belief system that drives their behavior" to make decisions about their work, and inspire them to invest in the renewed future of the organization.

A story I heard a number of years ago exemplifies this concept perfectly. While a well-known leader in quality was consulting at the NASA organization, he found that everyone was happy and enthusiastic about their jobs—even the janitorial staff. Fascinated, he approached one gentleman and asked, "Why are you are so happy coming to work every day?"

The janitor replied that it was because he had such an important job. To which the consultant said, "You are a janitor; you sweep floors and empty waste baskets."

"No," the janitor said. "I am part of the team that is going to put a man on the moon."

Clearly, NASA had captured the power of having a vision, which it had properly articulated and communicated throughout the organization. A well-articulated vision statement will result in new and invigorated working relationships and employee loyalties.

*Please do this for me.* Go to a number of your employees and ask them to tell you (without them looking at a poster or card) what the true vision of your organization is.

## The Importance of Values[2]

Values give meaning to life and work, and provide fulfillment. To consider values in the workplace is to probe the very reason people work and the belief system that drives their behavior.

Values represent our most basic fundamental beliefs. They are the principles that will arouse an emotional reaction if you perceive them to be threatened. They can also spur on our greatest achievements. If our work incorporates our values, we are likely to find that what we do is meaningful, purposeful, and important. Former service career counselor at Stanford University Anne Greenblatt writes, "When your work is aligned with your values, you tap into the 'fire within.' The highest achievements of people and organizations arise when people feel inspired to accomplish something that fits their top values."

Let's face it; we spend more time at work than in any other single activity, including sleeping. It is therefore crucial that the place where we work, a place that has the greatest potential to satisfy our basic needs, has a code of conduct that easily matches our primary values.

---

[2] *I will go into more detail regarding values in the chapter on Culture. At that time I will detail how to make them come alive in your organization and how to ensure all employees know how to make decisions based on the values of the organization. So my objective at this point is to just introduce the concept.*

*Bottom line:* If the people with whom we work do not respect our values, we will find another place to work. Conversely, if we do not respect or honor our organization's values, we will be asked to leave.

## Aligning Employee and Organizational Values

In my work as a trainer and management consultant, I meet with many corporations. Before these meetings, one of the first things I do is assess whether the corporation truly values its people. This assessment process typically starts when I enter the foyer of the building. I look around and frequently find framed posters of the organization's *vision* or *mission statement* that quite regularly contain a statement that says something like: "People are our number one resource."

I tell the corporation's leaders, "That's great! People should be your number one resource." Then I ask, "How often do you enroll your people in personal development programs, or let them get together at a conference so they can learn from each other and share experiences?" Unfortunately, some of them say, "We don't have time for that," or "It's not in the budget this year."

Then I point to vehicles in the parking lot, with the company name on the side, and ask, "Do you ever take your company trucks in for maintenance?" They usually reply, indignantly: "Certainly! We always ensure they are running efficiently, and safely." My response is, "In that case, you should change your statement to, "Trucks are our number one resource."

## Vision and Mission

I have introduced vision and mission, but I often notice that many teams become confused over the difference between the two. iLeaders and their teams should spend time and effort defining what they do (mission) and where they are going (vision). This will provide a sense of purpose and direction to the team, help to distinguish your team from others and describe your team's uniqueness, give your team a starting point for defining its strategies, goals, and structure. This all will become part of the basis for making critical and daily decisions.

Is it worth the time to define the mission and vision? You bet. Otherwise, you have a bunch of individuals working on their own goals and agendas. Just don't get bogged down in terminology. A statement or statements about what you do and where you are going is the "glue" that holds the team together.

## Defining Vision

An organization's *vision* represents their dream for the future. The vision, articulated with approximately five to ten words, is the beacon of light keeping the entire organization focused on the course to being a world-class supplier of its products or services in its area of expertise.

Some examples of great vision statements that fit the criteria of around five words and resulted in an organization's transformation include: "No Child in the World Shall Go to Bed Hungry" (Oxfam), "A Computer in Every Home" (Microsoft), and "Conquer Cancer In Our Lifetime" (Princess Margaret Hospital). Of course, one that was more than five words was President John F. Kennedy's: "...landing a man on the moon and returning him safely to the Earth." These are all visions that people can visualize. Once a vision is achieved, the organization moves on to a new and modified area of business focus.

Understanding the vision is not enough, however. iLeaders are able to inspire others towards that vision. This kind of inspiration not only involves their headspace, but their heart-space as well. It is important that employees have enthusiasm towards their profession, enjoy doing the work, and feel that it matters. A vision-driven organization recognizes that people truly want to succeed and want the organization to be successful.

As I mentioned earlier, some management teams seem more concerned about word-smithing and platitudes than then creating content that employees can relate to. This results in draining the energy from the team! When crafting the mission and vision, iLeaders allow their team to contribute to the main thoughts, words, phrases, and insights, and then let a few volunteer team members wordsmith the statement "off-line." This will save the entire team time and energy, and the team members will remain positive and committed to their purpose and direction.

## Defining Mission

The *mission statement* of an organization should answer the basic question, "What is the reason for our existence right now?" It should be only one sentence and articulate clearly the following items:

- What is it we do?
- For whom do we do it?
- Why do we do it?

I should be able to go to any employee at any level in the organization and ask, "What is the reason for your company's existence right now?" They should be able to respond, "The reason for our existence is to…" That is the mission: one sentence. Unfortunately for many organizations, the mission is often just a high-level platitudes and statements describing a desired working culture about how to interact with clients, or a plan to work on a daily basis, and does not inspire focused behavior.

In my seminars, I ask participants if they know the mission statements of highly successful organizations. They invariably answer "yes" and, surprisingly, many can state them. We then ask, "Does your organization have one?" About 50 percent raise their hands. We then ask, "Who here can state it right now?" Only about five percent are able to do this without referring to written material.

Can all employees in your organization articulate the mission without reading it?

Some common examples:[3]

**Metro Police**: *To serve and to protect.*
**Johnson and Johnson**: *To alleviate pain and disease.*
**Marriott**: *To make people away from home, feel at home.*
**Merck**: *To preserve and improve human life.*
**Disney Corporation**: *To provide happiness to millions and promulgate wholesome American values.*

## Strategic Objectives

After all this is established, a company determines its *strategic objectives*. These should be focused on the three key areas that will ensure long-term success for the organization. These are the following:

---

[3] *Some of the Vision and Mission examples used have since been updated.*

1. **Business Requirements** - measured in terms of revenue, margin, profit, market share, ROI, ROA, EBIDA, ROTA, revenue per employee, balanced scorecard and so on.

2. **Customer Satisfaction** - measured by client loyalty, repeat business, referrals, satisfaction surveys, testimonials, complaint letters, and so on.

3. **Employee Satisfaction** - also measured pragmatically in terms of loyalty, attrition, punctuality, morale, absenteeism, assessment surveys, and executive interviews.

Goal setting 101 tells us that objectives should be SMART (Specific-Measurable-Attainable-Realistic-Timely). It is surprising, but even today many organizations' goals fail this simple test.

These three basic areas of goals should always be kept in balance. If one succeeds at the expense of the others, it will ultimately become the Achilles heel of any organization. A company can make all kinds of money, but if the customers are inherently unhappy with the way they are being treated, the company will ultimately fail. Or, it could have the happiest customers in the country, but if the employees are significantly dissatisfied and leave, it will fail. On the other hand, the company could have the happiest employees in the world, but if it is not making the profits to pay bills and provide a return for shareholders, they will again fail.

To achieve all three criteria, every individual in the organization must play a part in the strategic planning process. Of course, the planning starts at the top. But then, all managers must be involved. After that, each unit, division, or department should cascade it down to all levels of employees. Everyone in the organization must have an opportunity to provide input or make comment.

If this is done correctly, the company will achieve empowerment. When this happens, there will be higher levels of unit productivity, effective managers who are not overworked or heading for burn-out, and lower attrition because employees are happier.

## The Crises of Transitions

Understanding the various phases that an organization will naturally evolve through is a good start. But there is more. At each estuary where the company transitions from one phase to another, there will be predictable crises that must be addressed. If they are ignored, then the organizations are likely to fail. If iLeaders address crises proactively, organizations will move constructively into the next phase.

## 1. Entreprenurial Phase & Transitional Solutions

When a business evolves from the Entrepreneurial Phase to the Bureaucratic Phase, the crisis is caused by complacency. This is natural, because the iLeader and their team has taken this organization from non-existence to a multimillion dollar business. iLeaders maintain an attitude of command and control. Perhaps thinking, *Who could teach us anything? Look what we have accomplished that no one else could!*

iLeaders by this point have experienced many big wins, and are not aware of how or why they now have to do business differently in order to maintain their company's momentum of success. The iLeader does not become arrogant or overconfident, and does not seek to live in the past.

iLeaders, when faced with the Entrepreneurial Phase crisis are self-actualized, decisive, competitive risk-takers. That is the approach necessary to turn their initial dream into reality. However, continuing that culture of "take big risks" and maintaining the decision-making process of ready—shoot—aim, which was great in start up, will not be a successful strategy as the company evolves.

Personal development in the early stages was focused on sales skills development, time management, and account management. Beyond that, however there was very little interest in investing in a higher level of education for staff. This is often because employees were handpicked and came from other organizations with solid experience and good track records.

## 2. Bureaucratic Phase & Transitional Solutions

In the Bureaucratic Phase, many long-term employees are heard walking the halls saying things like, "I remember the good old days around here," or, "I remember how you were treated like a human before this new management team took over."

Sometimes the reporting structures become a mile wide and a mile deep, reaching up to 16 levels of management. Then, customers often complain that the company is not in touch with their needs any more.

The crisis the organization experiences is one of uncertainty. This will happen because it has experienced major failure, and there are too many employees whose skills have become outdated and are just not what is required to grow the business to the next level. In addition, the product or service has become commoditized and there are other organizations that have comparable products and services, often at a more attractive price to the consumer.

In order to take their companies successfully through to the next phase, iLeaders are achievement-focused, process-oriented, and can work from a high-level vantage point.

During this crisis, some companies will go through a process of downsizing, rightsizing, and restructuring. Others break up into smaller entities in order to break down the bureaucracy, which is constipating growth.

### 3. Silo Phase & Transitional Solutions

In the Silo Phase, companies break up into smaller entities and the battle cry becomes, "get closer to the customer". These silos, whether they are called *lines of business, strategic business units, divisions,* or *functions*, are focused on a specific product line or service. The primary measurements at this phase are all the "R" words, such as E to R, ROI, ROA, ROCA, and so on.

Companies in this phase experience a couple of issues. One is a lack of communication. One silo may be making decisions that could significantly affect the others, but no one is informed. The other issue is that the silos are competing with each other for the customers' business. This becomes irritating to the customer and bad for the company as well.

If this goes on too long, the threat will become one of conflict. This happens because of turf wars and role confusion, individual managers wanting to become heroes and show each other up, and the fact that the company's products and services become commoditized. A sense of distrust pervades the workforce because it seems their biggest competitor is the sister silo.

An iLeader in the Silo Phase is affiliative, has strong technical skills, and is a good communicator. In order to address the issues of the Silo Phase, businesses reorganize themselves to bring the different factions together. So, instead of the silo being focused on a specific product or service, it must transition to focus on the customer.

## 4. Matrix Phase and Transitional Solutions

Now that the silos are organized by customer (whether it is customer size, geography or customer industry), one executive is in charge of "each specific" function across all silos. The Matrix Phase is designed to fix many of the issues in the silo phase. However, taken to extremes, it will cause the company to experience a crisis of despair, because too many managers are looking at the same indicators and measurements. For example, in the matrix phase, one of the primary measurements is EBITDA (Earnings Before Interest, Income Tax, Depreciation and Amortization).

An iLeader in the Matrix Phase must be very humanistic, a divergent thinker, and seek to understand and empathize with issues across all functions.

## 5. Empowerment Phase & Transitional Solutions

Those companies that are able to evolve into the Empowerment Phase will enjoy great success and strong employee engagement. They implement the Balanced Scorecard as their primary measurement focus.

However, for a number of years, the culture has been touted as the be-all and end-all. But it is not. This stage can be taken too far, and the organization will become complacent again. This happens because authors write about them, quality gurus use them as examples, and TV documentaries praise their virtues, so they become overconfident. Their success actually becomes their weakness. Think of Toyota; it was an organization that really excelled in the Empowerment Phase. However, during the quality crises they have been experiencing, they remained arrogant and focused more on denying rather than resolving issues.

An iLeader in the Empowerment Phase is self-actualized, maintains a high level of trust in others, has an affiliative mindset, and is truly comfortable delegating tasks to others.

# Where is your Organization?
## What crises will you be facing?

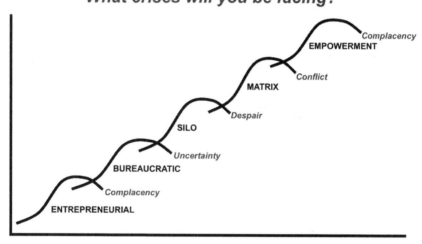

## Is there a Shortcut?

At this point, many executives ask me: Is it necessary to go through all of these steps, or can we go straight to a collaborative organization? Unfortunately, there is no shortcut. Each of these phases must be experienced. The only thing that can be mitigated is how long the transition takes, and how deep the crises go. But, by actually experiencing each of these phases, the organization can become stronger.

It took IBM 60 years to go through these phases. It took General Motors 80, and even then only a few units made it to the Empowerment Phase. It took Microsoft 25 years, and maybe Google 15 years. But, every organization will eventually go through each of these phases.

Unfortunately, they will not go through the phases in a linear fashion, as I have laid this out. What usually happens is the company will go from Entrepreneurial to Bureaucratic, and then back to Entrepreneurial, then up to Silo, then back to Bureaucratic, and so on. Often, a company will get into an endless loop until it dies or is bought out or merged with some other organization.

Business owners should be aware that the leaders who caused the company to be successful in the Entrepreneurial Phase may not be the right leaders to take it through the Bureaucratic Phase. The leader who was successful in the Bureaucratic Phase may cause the company to fail in the Matrix Phase.

## What Comes Next?

I believe we are entering into an age where there will be more non-full-time employees, such as independent contractors, part-time workers, retired second career people, and lots of outsourced workers. I see them as free-floating neurons bouncing around the occupational cortex and moving from organization to organization on a regular basis.

My good friend and futurist, Warren Evans, has coined a phrase for this. He calls it "Hollywood Days and Cyber Nights." He explains it this way:

The Hollywood days refer to the way Hollywood works. When someone decides to make a movie they bring together actors, sound technicians, costume designers, and so on. When the movie is completed everyone goes their own way. Somewhere else, somebody else is making a movie and needs actors, costume designers, producers, and directors. So they come together again to make a movie, and again each goes their own way.

The cyber nights refer to the fact they we are all going to have to be wired 24/7. Anyone wanting to know where the opportunities are will need to be carrying a Blackberry, iPhone, iPad, laptop or some other communication device. It will become more important to be connected to LinkedIn, Facebook, Flicker, YouTube, Twitter, and so on. At the writing of this book, we are not sure how each of these social media alternatives will end up, as with all new concepts. There will be a shakeout and only a few will rise to the top.

However, don't waste time trying to predict which it will be. Just get connected. Flip a coin if you have to. Anyone who says the new technologies and social networking are not important reminds me of my dad. When I was three years old we lived in a farmhouse with no electricity or telephone. My mom wanted a telephone. I can still remember Dad saying, "Why would anyone need a telephone? If you want to talk to someone, you just go visit them."

I know of 80- and 90-year-olds who are now using much of the latest technology – with great enthusiasm.

The biggest cause of stress and foundation of most employee discontentment is that we are still working in an antiquated corporate structure and using management processes designed for an industrial age.

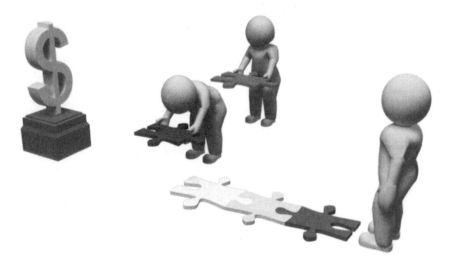

# iLeader Profile

## *Murray Smith*

*Entrepreneur Murray Smith's passion is to ignite and unite the entrepreneurial spirit to achieve extraordinary results. He is the bestselling co-author of* The Answer *and responsible for the resurrection of the Indian Motorcycle brand.*

When Murray was young, his family was told that he had a learning disability and would never amount to much. After repeating a year in school and continuing to fail, he was pulled out of the public school system and sent to a school that was "equipped to handle his special needs." In other words, he went to a school for kids who couldn't make it in the regular system.

The expectation was that after finishing school, he would work in a factory, and that would be that. Sure enough, his first job was with Superior Sewer Services a company that put him to work cleaning sewers a hundred feet below the city streets. He felt that was an accurate reflection of his worth.

But in his heart he didn't want to live a below-average life; he didn't even want to live an *average* life. His desire was to create financial freedom for himself, and that this was never going to happen as long as he had a menial job. He realized something else too: The two guys who were running that sewer company were no smarter than he was. They just focused on the few critical things needed to increase revenues.

He eventually left the sewers and went to work at a factory called Supreme Aluminum where he operated a metal press making kettles. He also worked at a number of other jobs, none of them being very exciting. But again, he realized the owners were no smarter than him. Yet they were all successful. He also noticed they focused on similar activities to the guys who owned the sewer company and what was critical to increasing revenues.

Murray continued to accept jobs that reflected what he was repeatedly told was his level of ability, until a moment came when something inside shifted, and he took a radically different course.

He was working for Bell Canada at the time, a $50 billion company, which at the time was the largest telephone company in the world. He was a cable-puller, one of the guys who went out and installed phone systems for business customers. During those years at Bell, he heard a lot of customers complain about the exorbitant rates that came with a monopoly. *"If only there were some competitive companies"*, he heard them grumble. After continually hearing that, he asked, "If I started my own phone company, would you do business with me?" The answer always came back: "Yes."

When deregulation came to the telecom industry in 1979, Murray saw his opportunity. He didn't know anything about how to run a large business, let alone how to start one. However, he had something most of his co-workers didn't: a genuine passion for what he was doing. He realized that better phone service would improve the quality of people's lives, so he greeted that opportunity with a commitment to provide outstanding work. And he knew the telephone industry.

The market was hungry for a competitive service. Murray thought to himself, *I could keep working as an employee, earning low wages, or I could provide that competitive service as the owner of a telecom business.* So, at the age of 20, he left Bell and started his own telephone company.

All the messages Murray had been conditioned with for twenty years had fostered a belief that he would never amount to much. He believed differently and did not buy into that crap. That compelling desire was too strong to be contained. He knew in his bones that it was time to recondition his brain and build a new belief. The process he put himself through was what we now describe in our industry as *neural reconditioning*. At the time, he didn't know that's what he was doing – he just did it.

The string of experiences that took Murray Smith from sewer worker to boardroom executive taught him something that would change the course of his life: Building a successful business is not rocket science. He saw plenty of people in business who were academically accomplished, brilliant, who knew *stuff*, intellectually, than he may ever know. But they weren't running these companies, and often they were not the ones living their dreams, either.

Murray thought success in business was his ticket to the better life he envisioned, and knew the path to that success was not in academic achievement: It was in figuring out the critical components of running a business — any business — and learning how to make those components work together correctly. So he said to himself: *"I can do that."*

It occurred to Murray that perhaps what people had called his "disability" was just a different way of looking at things. Many people operate very effectively based on their intuitions. For Murray, it's almost the opposite. His brain processes information in a very compartmentalized way. He doesn't read a lot; in fact he has only ever read one book.

He does not spend a lot of time in theoretical or abstract thought. He is at his best when working methodically, analytically and strategically with a concrete, tangible process in front of him. He has always had a very no-nonsense, bottom-line view of life, and found that he could hone this perspective into a unique ability to look at businesses, quickly diagnose their problems, and figure out how to fix them.

## The School of Hard Knocks

Murray's new phone company, Alternative Communications, Inc. (trade name: Altel), become Bell's first competitor, and he stayed in that business long enough to taste success.

This was not an easy time in Murray's life. In addition to competing against the largest phone company in the world, a slew of telecom giants from the United States, Europe and Asia also showed up to do battle on this newly competitive turf. However, Murray's group was more determined than were prepared. They experienced plenty of tough challenges.

Several years later, his marriage had fallen apart. But by this time he had learned quite a bit about business. Now a single dad with a seven-month-old daughter, he walked away with more experience than money so spent the next few years as an employee, once again.

Murray was now working as a charter employee of a new company, Telecommunications Terminal Systems (TTS), which had a plan to build the first national telecom company in Canada that spanned all provinces. Until that time, each province had been regulated independently.

He helped the company accomplish this by creating a national dealer division, which resulted in building revenues to about $60 million.

It was then when he looked at what he was doing. There he was, helping someone *else* make money. So he decided to go into business for himself, for the second time.

He created a company called New Opportunities Corporation (NewCo), which looked for promising new technologies to develop. One of the first companies they became involved with was a venture that was revolutionizing the digital storage of audio information. Have you ever stopped in front of a home and noticed a box on the "For Sale" sign that said to tune in to a local FM radio station for more information? You have just seen one of their products. They ended up owning two national FM broadcast licenses in Canada and the U.S., and worked out deals with real estate companies, airports, and MacDonald's.

NewCo evolved into an incubator company that worked with new ventures in media, technology, engineering, import, energy management, manufacturing, and more. They were similar to an investment company, but in addition to financial backing, they took an active role in running each company, including its management and marketing.

After running NewCo for five years, Murray consulted with a $350 million media company that owned 26 radio stations, 30 or so magazines, and 50-plus TV stations. He worked with them for two years, building a place-based media division. He then moved on, forming a partnership with a group that owned a private television network. You've probably had the experience of waiting to board a plane and watching the airport's television network on monitors at your gate; theirs was the first company in America to provide that kind of private television network.

By this time Murray had clearly established a pattern: He never stayed at any of these business adventures for longer than a few years, through that critical Entrepreneurial Phase. He wasn't really interested in carving out a career in any one industry, or in running any of these companies long-term. What did interest him was figuring out *how to run* them, taking them from wherever they were, setting them on a track to success, and then moving on to learn more.

After working in industries including telecom and technology to network marketing and personal development, Murray applied and honed his approach in a wide range of fields. It was now time to put it to the test. Now he wanted to take on the challenge of building something huge, from the ground up.

## Indian Motorcycle

Murray has always been a passionate motorcycle enthusiast. In 1994, he purchased an Indian Motorcycle T-shirt and thought, "Too bad . . . this used to be a great brand." In its day, Indian Motorcycle was bigger than Harley Davidson, but it had closed its doors in 1953. Yet the brand had been so compelling that even now, after languishing in bankruptcy for nearly half a century, it still had the power to evoke a compelling sense of quality and identity.

The thought he had about Indian when he bought that T-shirt in 1994 was stored away in his unconscious brain, along with countless millions of others. When he was ready, the Law of Attraction brought the thought to his conscious attention. In 1997, three years after buying that T-shirt, he got a call from a friend, Rick Genovese, who told Murray there was an opportunity to buy into a company that owned the rights to the clothing company for Indian. He described the strategy that would be required to pull this venture off successfully; Rick listened, thought about it, and decided he wasn't interested. But Murray knew this was a project that could be viable. He immediately put together a consortium and made a bid on the Indian Motorcycle name.

### Belief Will Always Trump Logic

At the time, there were a dozen other bidders for the trademark, including groups with far more clout, money and power than they had. Nobody believed that this little group from Canada had even a ghost of a chance. But they had a different belief—and their belief prevailed over the odds. The bid was accepted and they now owned the coveted Indian Motorcycle brand.

Before opening, they spent a full six months doing nothing but evaluating and strategizing, following the exact same processes I have written about in this book. They figured out precisely who the ideal client was, how to uniquely position the company and what sales process would identify the ideal clients. Also, they decide on which business models were optimal for them, and what strategies and tactics best fit their particular business model.

Murray hired five presidents who reported directly to him. Each one was responsible for the success of their respective divisions (Hospitality, Apparel, Licensing, Manufacturing and Parts & Service). It was imperative that everything they did satisfied all objectives and the larger vision. As well, it was important that everything was in alignment with their personal goals and values.

Most of all, they needed to be confident they had identified all the critical components that would ensure the master plan *worked*. It was important not to get bogged down in complexity—that they operated at all times with a clear view of the bigger picture. They transformed that larger vision into clear focus, and that their focus always translated into the critical actions that would catapult Indian Motorcycle into stratospheric success. Indian Motorcycle was positioned as a lifestyle brand that appealed to men women and children and was not just a motorcycle manufacturer.

When doors finally opened, the Indian brand came out blazing. They opened the first Indian Motorcycle Cafe & Lounge, a 30,000-square-foot complex that included a five-star restaurant, a nightclub, a lounge, a retail store, and featured new and vintage motorcycles throughout the facility. Then they opened two more Indian Motorcycle Lounges, put the clothing line into 800 retail outlets, produced a line of 450 licensed Indian Motorcycle products, and launched a worldwide network of Indian Motorcycle dealerships.

And of course, they built motorcycles. Did they build motorcycles! They found a partner who owned a custom motorcycle manufacturing company called California Motorcycle. So, rather than starting a new manufacturing arm from scratch, they paid this partner $20 million, took California Motorcycle, and changed its name to Indian Motorcycle. They built a half-million-square-foot, fully robotic manufacturing plant in Gilroy, California, the garlic capital of the world. Bikes were put into 250 motorcycle dealerships. They also opened a parts-and-services division. In addition to the regular Indian-branded line, they also built a few thousand custom motorcycles and established a private-branded division that built a thousand private-labelled machines.

In the first year, they generated $75 million and now had a company valued at $300 million. They became the largest employer in Gilroy and went on to become the second-largest U.S.-based motorcycle company in the world.

The Indian Motorcycle success story drew significant media attention, and was featured on CBS, NBC, and CNN, in Forbes Magazine, in thousands of newspapers, radio and TV stations and magazines globally, and on 2000 web sites in 70 countries. Murray Smith became a celebrity.

*In May 2000 Murray suffered a significant heart attack on an airplane and subsequently left Indian Motorcycle. He also suffered full cardiac arrest and spent a couple of months in the hospital recovering. He was told once again that his life would not be normal. As a result of significant oxygen deprivation he would be severally brain damaged and would not be capable of functioning without help.*

*Again, Murray chose not to listen to the doctors and began his own recovery plan by learning how to recondition his brain to compensate for loss of memory and brain function. After a year he decided to resurrect another heritage motorcycle brand named American Motorcycle.*

*Now Murray focuses his amazing talents on helping other people overcome their barriers to success and apply the strategies that he knows will transform people's businesses and lives. He is presently involved with a growing number of companies and initiatives dedicated to helping small business owners and professionals thrive.*

# Summary

## *Chapter One*

## The Evolving Work Environment

**1.** *The Entrepreneurial Phase.*
**2.** *The Bureaucratic Phase.*
**3.** *The Silo Phase.*
**4.** *The Matrix Phase.*
**5.** *The Empowerment Phase.*

## The Strategic Plan

❧ *Establishing values and vision.*

❧ *Creating a mission.*

❧ *Implementing strategic objectives.*

## Preparing for Transformational Crises

**1.** *Avoiding entrepreneurial burnout.*
**2.** *Bypassing bureaucratic constipation.*
**3.** *Harnessing the conflict of silos.*
**4.** *Understanding the confusion of the matrix.*
**5.** *Making empowerment work.*

## What Can Be Done

❧ *Creating an* intra-*preneurial mindset.*

❧ *Developing effective systems.*

❧ *Becoming market-focused.*

❧ *Collaborating cross-functionality.*

# Chapter Two

## *Motivating the Team*

*"Your most precious possession is not your financial assets. Your most precious possession is the people you have working there, and what they carry around in their heads, and their ability to work together."*
- Robert Reich

The most important asset in any organization is not one that is on the balance sheet. The asset most critical to the future success of any business is the people, and their ability to work together.

It is not completely obvious to the casual observer, but we in North America are about to experience workplace diversity that has no parallel in history. Over the years we have had many different generations of workers — large groups who shared characteristics and attitudes towards work and life. Let's start by looking at the "early to bed, early to rise" Traditionalists.

## Traditionalists

Those workers born before 1945 were the very loyal and dutiful workers, who showed up on time every day, often went home for lunch, or carried a lunchbox and thermos, put in a good day's work, and went home to their family life each evening. Most of them men, they could be recognized by the pocket protectors in their shirts, patches on their elbows, and spats on their shoes. Many were raised on farms or with working class families and lived through the lean years of the Great Depression. Decades later, eating a nice thick steak for dinner, or having a $100 bill in their wallet, were signs to them of great prosperity.

They were civic-minded people, loyal to their country and employer, often working for the same company all their lives. This group has almost entirely retired from the work force. Some early Baby Boomers from more remote or rural areas also have the same working attitude as the Traditionalists.

## Baby Boomers

Then along came the Baby Boomers, so called because of the explosion in the birth rate after World War II, averaging four million births per year between 1946 and 1964. They rebelled against everything the Traditionalists stood for, and rejected their frugal values. Collectively, these Baby Boomers have made up a very significant portion of the workforce for a long time. In total, over 70 million of them have made their way through the workforce. But now, they are entering retirement years by the millions, which will cause a shortage of workers in many critical professions.

## Gen X

The third wave in today's workforce is Gen X, born between 1965 and 1979. They are a smaller group, not joiners, and many are the early adopters of the newer technologies. Without a distinct identity as a generation or group, they are seen as facing an uncertain, ill-defined future. They are the generation who became primarily known, as the Traditionalists might say, "for openly sleeping together before they got married."

They stopped going to churches, and did not sign up for memberships in non-profit organizations. But, they did give lift to the whole wave towards fitness clubs, and healthy eating.

## Gen Y

The next group is Gen Y, born after 1980. Like Gen X, this group is not significant in numbers. They are very comfortable using technology as part of their work and life, and changed the way we view and contribute to our jobs on a day-to-day basis. When the doctor cut their umbilical cord, the mother put a cell phone in their child's hand and they were connected forever. The cell phone or smart phone has now become the world's longest umbilical cord. As well, their communication is based on 140 characters or less.

## Millennials

A sub-group of the Y generation referred to as the Millennials (born after 1990) is currently coming into the workforce by the millions. So, you better get to know them, and fast. Why? Because they (combined with the Boomers) are going to cause some of the most dramatic changes in our working culture.

You see, the Millennials grew up in Mr. Rogers' neighborhood. And in Mr. Rogers' neighborhood, everyone is special. They believe they are special, just because we told them they were special.

Some of you may recall Boomers were considered special too. They were special if they came home with an "A" on their report card. Or, if they got a summer job. Or, if they hit a home run. Alas, not in Mr. Rogers' neighborhood. In Mr. Roger's neighborhood, you didn't even have to play in the game and you came home to your parents with a trophy. The reasoning is that no child should be left out, or their self-esteem deflated, no matter how much effort they did or did not contribute.

The other thing you have may heard about this generation is that they were raised by *helicopter parents* — moms and dads who hovered nearby, watching, encouraging, protecting, and managing all aspects of their children's lives. So, if little Johnnie got into trouble at school, for instance, it was never Johnnie's fault. It had to be the teacher, or the system was not treating him properly. The parents would quickly go to the school and "fix" the problem.

Now these young Millennials are entering the workplace by the millions. And it should be no surprise to you that they continue to believe they should be treated as though they're special. I have worked with companies that do performance evaluations with employees, and when one of these young workers did not get an evaluation they believe they were entitled to, the manager actually received a visit from the parent, claiming that "Johnny" was not being treated fairly and that the manger must be picking on him.

Helicopter parents like this will insist on a satisfactory resolution, and they may even bring a lawyer.

With Millennial workers, there is a more important issue than hovering parents. They do not want jobs! Nevertheless, they do want to be engaged in meaningful work. They want to provide that work in an organization that has a collaborative culture, with a high standard of ethics...for about 18 months or so. Then they want to hike around Costa Rica.

When I tell this to executives, they often say, "Well, they'd just better learn." Unfortunately for those managers, the Millennials do not have to learn, and here's why: The group who will be filling labor and skill shortages in many industries will be the Baby Boomers. They are now coming back into the workforce as ROCs (Retirees on Call). They are often independent consultants, part-time workers, and contractors who want to work at their own schedule and take Alaskan cruises when they want.

So here we will have two completely different generations of workers, with opposite education, opposite technical skills, opposite experiences growing up, and very different work ethics, but with a mindset and approach to work that is exactly the same. And here, in the middle, are the other generations still trying to manage people the way they have been managed for the last 30 or 40 years. Unfortunately, this will simply not work anymore.

This new polarized work group environment will redefine the kind of culture that will function productively in the near future. More importantly, it will increase the time and effort all managers will have to expend in order to coach employees and try to keep them engaged.

## Motivating Millennials

Here are just a few of the important things necessary to encourage and reinforce human performance:

1. **Scrap the annual performance appraisal and provide regular constructive feedback.**

   - Provide a framework: Tasks must have daily, weekly or at most, monthly due dates.

   - Jobs will have to be structured in a way that will enable a balanced work life.

   - Meetings must have a purpose, be preceded by an agenda, and followed up with minutes.

   - Outcomes must be clearly articulated and daily progress reviewed.

2. **They require direct and ongoing coaching.**

   - Millennials have needs similar to the Traditionalists in that they want to learn from you and receive ongoing feedback.

   - They want to be "in" and involved with the big picture. Supervisors will be required to spend a lot of time instructing, coaching and mentoring. They will expect more of your time in helping them succeed.

3. **Their optimistic outlook must be encouraged.**

   - Millennials have an inflated personal self-image and are ready to take on the world.

   - Media hype told them they can do it – so they believe they can.

- Encourage them. Don't try to insist they learn reality.

4. **They work most effectively in a collaborative culture.**

   - Take advantage of the Millennials' ability to work in the true team spirit. Encourage this. They grew up working in groups and teams.

   - In contrast to the every-person-for-themselves attitude of earlier generations, Millennials actually believe a team can be more effective — they've experienced team success. It's not just related to age — watch who joins the volleyball match at the company picnic; Millennials gather in groups and play on teams.

   - Your coaching must become more team-centered.

5. **Truly listen to Millennials.**

   - Millennial employees grew up with doting parents who have scheduled their lives around the activities and events of their children.

   - These young adults have ideas and opinions of their own, and don't take kindly to having their feelings ignored. After all, they had the best listening, most child-centric audience in history.

6. **They love to be challenged.**

   - These workers love challenge and change.

   - Doing the same thing day after day is bad. They need variety.

- "What's next?" is always on their mind.
- They become bored easily and require constant attention.

## 7. Multitasking will be the norm.

- These new employees are multitaskers in a way you've never seen before. They are able to talk on the phone while doing email and answering multiple instant messages and eating lunch! This is now a way of life.

- Without many different tasks and goals to pursue within the week, the Millennials will likely experience boredom.

## 8. They were born to text.

- Take advantage of their ability to multi-task.
- They have been playing with video games, computers, and cell phones from birth. The electronic capabilities of these employees are amazing.
- The good news is, they actually like it when you stay in touch by texting. That way you can be updated real-time how it is going with a client.

## 9. Social media networking is their life.

- Capitalize on their comfort with electronic networking.
- In addition to being comfortable working in teams, millennial employees like to network with friends around the world. Keep this in mind, because

they are able to post their resume electronically to be viewed by millions of potential employers any time they wish.

- As I said, they are loyal. But, will keep their options open—always.

- A just plain stupid policy for an organization employing Millennials would be to ban or severely restrict Facebook, Twitter and other social media activity at the office.

## 10. Work-life balance will be the standard.

- Allow them time to volunteer for special causes.

- Get used to the fact they may play on sports teams, walk for multiple causes, spend time as fans at company sports leagues, and spend lots of time with family and friends.

- They will work hard, but not participate in the 60-hour workweeks in corporate cages practiced by Baby Boomers. Spending time at home, with family, and friends are priorities.

- Mixing personal and business activities is important to these Millennial Employees. Ignore this at your peril.

## 11. They demand a fun, employee-centered workplace.

- Millennials will select professions based on their talents, and they will want a workplace they enjoy. Their network of friends will probably be centered around the workplace.

- If your Millennial employees aren't laughing, going out with workplace friends for lunch, and helping plan the next company event or committee there may be a problem.

Now that you know what to expect from your Millennial employees and how valuable they can be to your organization, you can and should educate your other long-term employees on how to interact with the Millennials.

### Boomers will require special treatment also

To attract and retain the best and brightest of the Boomers who will be returning to the workforce, organizations need to change many existing policies and practices. Some practices that organizations will have to look at seriously are such things as creating a more flexible workplace. This will include programs like:

- Job-sharing
- Self-funded Leave of Absence (LoA)
- Phased-in retirement plans
- Shorter work weeks with longer days
- Part-time consultants and contract employees.

Some interesting statistics have come from recent studies:

- Older workers are 7% less likely to be absent.
- They do not fear change (they fear discrimination).

- Health is not determined by age, but by lifestyle.

I have heard it said many times that people do not like change. That is cow-paddy! People love change. They change their clothes, their cars, their houses, and sometimes even their wives or husbands.

People accepting change is not the problem. The problem is letting go of old stuff. Think of it. Who has a problem buying a new pair of shoes? More people have a problem throwing out the old ones. That is where our issue is. We need to stop doing old stuff. We are especially attached to behaviors that have either brought us success or made us comfortable in the past.

*"It is not the strongest of the species that survive, nor the most intelligent, but the one most responsive to change."*
- Charles Darwin

Change is tiring, and human beings can only tolerate so much in a given period of time. There was a study written up in the *Journal of Personality and Social Psychology* in 1998, at a mid-western university that illustrates this very well.

One evening, an experimenter phoned a group of students. She was studying people's preferences for various foods that they would be taste-testing.

The next morning, the students were escorted into her laboratory, which smelled of freshly baked cookies. She seated everyone at tables, each holding a plate of chocolate chip cookies and a plate of radishes.

Half the students were asked to taste-test the radishes and not even touch the cookies. The others got to eat the cookies and not the radish. She left them alone in the room. The students followed her instructions to the T. None of the radish-eating students touched the cookies, and vice versa.

Then the experimenter returned and said, "I wonder if I can ask you all a favor? A friend of mine is having trouble recruiting subjects for his study on solving puzzles. Could you help him out?" The students agreed. They were then introduced to the second experimenter. He took them to his lab and asked them to trace a complex figure without lifting their pens off of the paper or doubling back on themselves. If they accidentally did either of these things, they were to start over. He asked them to continue until they solved the puzzle or gave up. He started a stopwatch and they began.

You should realize the puzzle was impossible to solve. However, the subjects who had eaten the cookies were able to persist longer at the unsolvable puzzle than did subjects who had eaten the radishes.

Why did this happen? Because it takes energy to control willpower. After a while, people's willpower and focus become drained. When this happens, people give in.

This study and others like it show that people only have so much willpower. When people need to maintain control and optimism for a long period of time, their psychic energy runs out.

## Corporate Change

Our workforce is changing as well, which is frustrating for many of the older workers. The new generations of workers are no longer looking myopically at traditional job opportunities. They are looking inwardly, at themselves, to see what they can create. Gone are the days Boomers grew up in, when they were told, "Go to school and get good marks. If you get good marks you'll pass, and if you pass 12 or 13 times in a row you'll graduate, then get a job where you'll work until the age 65." Then receive their gold watch, retire – then die.

As generations continue to mix in the workplace, many older workers are reporting to younger bosses. A Career-Builder survey finds that 43% of workers ages 35 and older said they currently work for someone younger than themselves. Workers reported that there are a variety of reasons why working for someone younger than them can be a challenge, including:

- They act like they know more than me when they don't.

- They act like they're entitled and didn't earn their position.

- They micromanage.
- They play favorites with younger workers.
- They don't give enough directions.

Other research on older workers concludes:

- They are 7% less likely to be absent or ill.
- They are intrinsically motivated to perform, not for competitive reasons.
- Health is not determined by age, but by lifestyle.
- There are fewer demands on their time.

Rosemary Haefner, Vice President of Human Resources and Senior Career Advisor at CareerBuilder.com aptly notes as the economy began to emerge from the current financial crisis: "As companies emerge from this recession, it is important for employees to work together and move the business forward, regardless of their age."

There is also a connection between age and self-employment. Statistics Canada shows that the increase in self-employment was entirely concentrated among older workers, especially those aged 55 and over.

Each year, businesses will have to compete with an increasing number of opportunities for older, skilled workers who are becoming self-employed, as the Internet and other channels make entrepreneurship more profitable and possible for individuals across North America.

## A QUILT MADE OF PATCHES

The "Quilting Bee" has been a North American custom for many generations. Over the winter months, the women in a particular area would focus on developing, designing, and creating the most beautiful fabric patches they possibly could. Into each patch, they would pour their skills, focus, passion, and high-quality work to ensure that each patch was of the highest standards. Women who had great patches would then be invited to a Quilting Bee where they would go to work on pulling all of the patches together into a quilt.

If you were able to peek in through the window of a house where this was taking place, you would observe some very interesting behaviors. What you would *not* observe would be some *boss* quilt-lady telling participants *where* to place their patch, *when* to take a break, *what* the rules were, or *who* should do which task.

What you *would* observe would be all members working in the format of a "team", demonstrating *real* team behavior. They would be communicating with each other in a positive manner. They would be socializing; interested in each other's work, and automatically step in to help each other without being asked. But most of all, they would be focused on helping each other's work look better.

If you continued to observe, when the first woman would put down her patch, the second might come with hers and say, "The colors in my patch bring out and enhance the colors in your patch." Then the third may come with hers and say, "The design in my patch brings together and enhances the pattern in your patches."

Why were they doing this? Well, they had a vision, and that was to create the most beautiful quilt in the county. To confirm that this had been achieved, they may have entered it in the fall fair with a mission to win a blue ribbon. But whether they did this or not, they all knew there was only one way they could capitalize on each of their talents and create a beautiful piece of art, and that was to continually help make each other's work easier and better looking.

## Blue Ribbon

My past experience in working with many corporations is that in order for you to win a blue ribbon (which may be an employee of the month award, or manager of the year award) you must ensure that other people's patches (or work) do not look as good as yours. You most certainly were not motivated to help anyone else look like a better employee than you.

This is an old paradigm from the Industrial Age. It will not work anymore. iLeaders see the advantage in having their workforce use the Quilting Bee model and having employees come to work and sincerely try to help each other in their jobs, help others look better, and make others' work easier.

Think of your own organization. What if everyone in your company came to work each day with one thing in mind: What can I do today to help someone else have a better day? Or, how can sales make administration's job a little easier? How can administration make shipping's job a little easier? How can shipping make the salespeople's work a little easier? And so on.

Winona Ryder best articulated how this can be made to work in the movie *How To Make An American Quilt* (1995), when her character said while creating a quilt:

> *You must have a theme based on culture. You have to choose your combinations carefully. The right choices will enhance your quilt. The wrong choices will hide original colors and dull their beauty. There are no rules to follow; you have to go by instinct, and you have to be brave.*

This is how the truly successful organizations are going to be working in the future. Some of the clients I've worked with are already using this Quilting Bee model. Even in sales functions, they are modifying compensation programs to include what employees have done to help others in their work.

There are many inhibitors to successfully implementing this in an organization. One major inhibitor is a company not having a very straightforward strategic plan. Companies who want to implement a true teamwork model must have a clearly articulated set of values, a crisp vision that everyone can picture, a detailed mission to which people are committed, and a set of strategic objectives which are seen as attainable by the employees.

## Let go... of old attitudes and thinking

How we are going to have to work in the future is different than how we have worked in the past. Like it or not, we are heading into a whole new work environment where the contract between employees and employers has been rewritten, and the ways in which employees work together must be more symbiotic. Everyone in the organization must be educated in the ways the rules have changed.

As my friend Jim Clemmer states in his popular book *Growing the Distance,* "The popular goals of security, stability, and predictability are deadly. The closer we get to these dangerous goals, the more our growth is stunted and learning reduced. In today's quickly evolving world, if we fail to transform, it is we who will be changed out."

It has been said that when Einstein was teaching at Harvard, a student went to him and asked why he used the same exam questions as last year. Einstein replied, *"Because the answers have all changed."*

It is important that all managers react to the new working culture in a positive, productive attitude and an open mind.

We are all too familiar with the shifts in the marketplace and the subsequent impact on people in the workplace. Employers are looking for staff who will add value; they are thirsting for solution-oriented individuals who can help them solve a problem or improve their operations.

iLeaders harness the collective potential of all their employees. By doing this, they create the most powerful force against their competitors. To do this, however, involves teamwork. Unfortunately, the journey to build a cohesive team is fraught with difficulties. Some individuals resist because, to them, it appears they will lose control. Others resist because they assume the switch is just another fleeting passion for executives with too much time on their hands.

*A company's growth and very survival depends on how quickly and efficiently its people transform.*

The future is seen as both frightening and enlightening. We all live in the prison of our own paradigms. Over the years, our minds have been programmed to look at the world a certain way, to see others a certain way, and more importantly, to see ourselves through these same filters. It is something we all learn to live with, but we must escape.

I am currently doing extensive work in the Canadian prison system. I see people who are physically locked up and restrained. However, I believe that a mind closed to transformation, change and growth is the most unfortunate prison of all.

## Prisoners of Our Own Paradigms

Many managers still strongly resist new technologies. It is important that people of all ages adapt to things like the internet, e-mail, e-commerce, iPods, iPhones, iLearning, iConferences, social networking, and so on. An interesting statistic is that the biggest group adopting new technology just happens to be the Baby Boomers, many of whom are in their 60s. When I hear of people who are still resisting web technologies, I laugh. Soon enough, it will be the only way to purchase anything.

In the past when I suggested that everyone soon would be purchasing goods regularly from the Internet, many said, "Not me." But, now most will be. In fact, the things they own, like their vehicles, computers, refrigerators, phones, and houses, may be doing the on-line purchasing on their behalves. We will soon have refrigerators automatically ordering our groceries, microwaves reading bar codes to determine cooking times, and cars with systems that determine service problems and automatically book appointments with the dealerships for repair (*whoops*, I think this is already happening). Many people are being dragged kicking and screaming into the future. I ask, "Why are you fighting the inevitable?"

iLeaders embrace change. Organizational transformation only happens when the culture allows everyone to believe there are infinite possibilities to achieve success.

It has been said that imagination is more important than knowledge. Knowledge is limited. Imagination can take you to the ends of the universe.

## The Transformation into Management

We have all heard that one of the most under-utilized resources in most organizations is the potential of their people. The primary reason for this is the way they are managed. Companies promote high-potential people who have proven themselves to be very capable of doing their jobs, whether it's in sales, manufacturing, administration, customer service, or whatever.

They get promoted into management, and instead of doing things and fixing problems, they must change their mindset to getting things done through others. Since they are so good at "doing" and have no experience or training with managing and delegating, they ignore the development of their people and burn themselves out trying to be a sleeves-rolled-up manager taking care of every detail as it comes up.

A 2011 Poll by DDI Research Group found the following:

- 11% of managers in US companies have had any formal management training.
- 20% said they were promoted into management because of their technical skills, not their management expertise.
- 29% were happy with the support they received from management.
- 57% had to learn management through the "sink or swim" trial and error method.

These figures are atrocious. We would not even hire somebody to clean our windows without training them. And organizations continue to make people responsible for other human beings with no training whatsoever!

Today's competitive pressures have forced every organization to re-examine its structure. Most now realize that they can't afford to continue to operate with layer upon layer of management. To succeed in the future, every organization must:

- Embrace job sharing.
- Be more flexible with flatter reporting structures.

- Have day-to-day decision making closer to the customer.

- Continuous improvement must be the culture.

- Harness the collective capabilities of everyone within the organization.

- Be faster in creating new ways of doing business.

The organization that can harness the collective potential of all its employees will create a most powerful force for developing long-term, positive growth.

## Organizational Behavior

Organizational psychologists have often attempted to compare animal behavior with human behavior, searching for a link between the animal jungle and the corporate jungle. The studies conducted have resulted in many interesting findings, which in turn have been used to explain the more primal side of change. Some have been especially helpful in illustrating management behavior.

In his book *The Babinski Reflex*, Philip Goldberg illustrates a number of these studies that have been used by authors, management consultants, corporate trainers, and motivational speakers, just to name a few, as metaphors for resistance to change. There are a few that are important metaphors for organizational behavior.

## The Monkey's Dilemma

Researchers went to South America to discover why a particular species of monkey had become extinct. Not long after beginning their studies, they were able to determine that it was the oldest species that had died off, while a number of the younger or newer species still survived.

As they delved into the reasons why this had happened they were able to determine some contributory factors. One was that the local people had for many years hunted and captured these monkeys in order to sell them to any interested buyer. Another factor was the method of capture, as well as the older monkeys' inability to adapt and change.

The process went as follows:

- The hunters put food in the knotholes of trees.

- The monkeys were attracted to this food and squeezed their hand into the knothole to grab the food.

- Unfortunately for the monkeys, as they put their hand around the food, causing them to form a fist, they couldn't get their hand out and retrieve the desired food.

- The diameter of their fist around the food was now larger than the knothole they had forced their hand into, and they were stuck as long as they refused to let go of the food.

- The monkeys that did not want to let go of the food were, of course, captured.

This species of monkey had been surviving in this jungle for thousands of years, through drought, hurricanes, floods, famines, and hard times. When food was very, very scarce, the only way they stayed alive was by finding food, like eggs and insects, in the knotholes of the trees. These rare food sources were often the only nourishment they could find to allow them to survive.

Whenever these same monkeys came across the food hidden in the knotholes they were unwilling to let go. However, some newer species of monkeys learned to let go and escaped. Their ability to adapt and change allowed them to survive as a species. Unfortunately, the older species, because of their years of history and conditioning, were unable to let go. As a result they were all eventually captured, and now they are extinct.

This similar effect has happened to many people in organizations. At the moment, they are all successful because of their behaviors. That's the good news. The bad news is, if they keep on doing what they have always done they will not continue to succeed.

I often hear highly motivated people say, "Yeah, but I'm not one of those old monkeys; I think differently, and I've come in here with some different ideas." History tells us, however, these same people have too often succumbed to the Pike Syndrome and conformed to the inertia of tradition.

## The Pike Syndrome

For those of you who fish, you know that to catch a pike (a big fish that eats other fish) the best way is to use a little fish, like a minnow, or a lure that resembles a little fish. It seems that some creative researchers used these aggressive fish in one of their experiments.

The researchers put a bunch of pike in a great big aquarium and then threw in some minnows. Predictably, the pike went though the tank like Pac-Man and ate all the little fish. Next, the researchers put the little fish into a large, clear glass jar and lowered the jar into the aquarium. As soon as the hungry pike saw the little fish they immediately swam towards them so that they might devour these delectable morsels. To their surprise, they bonked their noses on the invisible glass barrier. They couldn't see the glass; all they understood was that every time they went to eat the fish, they ended up with a sore nose.

After many unsuccessful tries to satisfy their hunger, the pike simply gave up. They stopped trying to get at the fish in the glass jar.

As soon as the researchers determined that the pike were reluctant to hurt themselves on this invisible barrier, they took the glass jar out of the aquarium and dumped all the minnows in to swim with the pike. The result was that even though the glass no longer protected the minnows, the pike made no attempt to eat them. The minnows could even swim right past the pikes' noses, and still the pike would not attack. They let the experiment go until all the pike starved, with their food swimming around in front of their noses.

This has happened to so many potentially great employ- ees. They get hired or promoted and come with a lot of great ideas, lots of enthusiasm and spirit, and then get bonked on the nose every time they present a new idea. This conditions them to believe that in order to survive, they should only show up and do their jobs—nothing beyond that. It happens to a lot of employees. It inhibits growth, development, creativity, and all of those things that enable an organization to reach its full potential.

This happens because of the way managers treat these new employees. I have often wondered why. Why do managers continue to treat staff the way they did 40 or 50 years ago? One of the answers to this comes from the book *The Babinski Reflex*. It goes like this.

## Eat Those Bananas

Often when experiments are done with monkeys, researchers use the Rhesus breed, since they have the DNA most closely linked to humans. In the following experiment, researchers placed a number of Rhesus monkeys in a room that was designed to meet their requirements. They were well fed and well cared for.

Once a day, every day, the researchers would lower a bunch of nice, fresh bananas through a hole in the ceiling. When the monkeys grabbed the bananas, their action tripped a switch that activated a nearby air conditioner. As a result, the monkeys received a blast of freezing, icy cold air. This shot of cold air was so uncomfortable for them that they released the bananas and scattered away from the offered treats.

The next day the researchers followed the same process. Again the monkeys scattered from the cold air, and so on; you get the idea. After a few days, some of the monkeys would not even go near the bananas when they appeared. Eventually, none of them would approach their favorite food. The researchers then deactivated the switch so it would no longer give the monkeys a cold blast. Afterwards, regardless of how many times the researchers lowered the bananas into the room, the monkeys would not attempt to approach or grab any of the bananas.

The interesting part of the experiment, however, is what happened next. After all the monkeys refused to approach the bananas, for fear of a cold blast of air, the researchers began to change their makeup of the group. Once a day, every day, they removed one monkey from the room and replaced it with a brand new monkey that had never experienced the cold blast of air.

They continued to lower the bananas into the room each day. Not only did the monkeys who had experienced the cold blast of air continue to avoid the bananas, but the newly introduced monkeys also avoided the lowered food. The researchers continued to replace the monkeys one by one, each day, until not one monkey in the room had ever experienced the cold blast of air. They continued to offer the bananas each day, and still, you probably guessed it, no monkeys went to take a banana.

If you could ask one of those monkeys, "Why don't you go and eat those bananas?" the monkey would probably look at you and say, "Well, that's just not the way it's done around here!"

How familiar is that statement? Have you ever heard a manager in your organization say something like, "You know, we tried that back in 1993. If I recall correctly, someone tried to sue us or something because of it, so we don't do that anymore. In fact, I think we now have a policy."

We see examples of this occurring in organizations where people are still using old practices. In some cases the reason the practice is in place is no longer valid. But these practices have become such an ingrained part of the culture that every new person coming in picks them up and does not question the rationale behind them.

*"The truth is that we can learn to condition our minds, bodies, and emotions to link pain or pleasure to whatever we choose. By changing what we link pain and pleasure to, we will instantly change our behaviors."*

- Anthony Robbins

## Managers Today

Sadly, many managers today behave the same way their managers did 40 and or 50 years ago — and it didn't even work that well back then. It sure isn't working any better today, yet they still continue to repeat the same behavior.

Perhaps we can't fault the researchers for assuming that we do at times behave like trained monkeys.

I will reinforce this with an old story that has been around for about 30 years. Perhaps some of you have heard this before. But I will provide an epilogue of my own.

It is the story about the woman preparing Easter dinner. Just before she was about to put the ham in the pot, she cut each of the ends off. Her 10-year-old daughter was watching and asked, "Mom, how come every time you cook a ham, you cut the ends off"? The mother said, "Because that is how you cook a ham." The daughter said, "But why?" "It makes it taste better," said the mother. The daughter continued to question her mother's practice. Finally, after several more questions, the mother said, "Look, I know it's the right way to cook a ham because that's the way Mother always did it."

So the daughter said, "Can we call grandma?" Which they did. The conversation went basically the same way, until the grandmother finally said, "That is the way my mother always did it." So, of course, the 10-year-old asked, "Can we call great-grandma?" and they did. After the girl asked her question, there was silence on the line. Finally the great-grandmother said, "Oh, my dears, I don't do that anymore. I just couldn't afford a pot big enough to hold the ham when your grandmother was growing up."

Many of you have heard this much, but there is more. A gentleman approached me after one of my sessions and claimed to be currently married to a woman who was the

10-year old girl in this story. He told me that her mother actually still cuts the ends off the ham. In spite of her new knowledge, she just could not "let it go." Her belief system said that the ham would taste better.

Research tells us that over 75% of all our day-to-day behaviors are based on conditioning—not our education, not our intelligence, not on our knowledge, or even our training.

## Intrinsic Motivation

Many leaders will resist giving up their carrots, and many employees will find it hard to imagine a world without incentives. But leaders who can inspire intrinsic motivation can expect a whole new workplace—and an entirely new definition of work.

Although intrinsic motivation is a fascinating theory, it is hard to relate to motivating employees in the workplace. So I came up with my own motivational hierarchy, which helped me to better understand what was happening. I discovered at the base of motivations for people who worked for me was the need to "get or keep a job," I found that new or potential employees would sincerely promise to do almost anything required, just for the opportunity to be hired or maintain their position.

However, once that need was confidently met, it also ceased to be a motivator, and employees went on to the next level, which I call "opportunity for growth and development." Or stated differently, what's in it for me (WIFFM). So when asked to go out of their way, perhaps working on a long weekend or assisting in an urgent situation, they wanted to know if their efforts would result in potential promotions or new and challenging projects. Once their need for growth and development was satisfied, it too ceased to be a motivator, and they went on to the next level, which is "peer respect."

At this point, employees performed primarily to impress and gain the recognition and respect of the people they worked with. When they gained that level, it would also cease to be a motivator, and they moved on to the next level, "recognition and respect from management." This is a strong and important need that must be satisfied in order for any employee to feel valued and develop a desire to succeed. When this need is met, an employee will go to the top of the pyramid of motivation, which is "personal achievement." This happens when an employee works at peak performance because of the self-satisfaction of successfully achieving goals and objectives. An illustration of this model follows.

*Personal Achievement*

*Recognition from Management*

*Respect from Peers*

*Opportunity for Growth & Development*

*Get or Keep a Job*

### *Sherren's Hierarchy of Motivation* ©

If any of these motivation factors are blocked, an employee will regress. For instance, if an employee feels secure in their job and ready to progress to the next level, but finds that growth and development are not possible, they will regress to the previous motivation level and go look for another job somewhere else.

Likewise, if the need for recognition and respect from management was blocked, the employee would continue to increase their need for respect from peers. This could manifest itself as a focus on getting together with other employees, having bitch sessions, and eventually turning other employees against the management. Ultimately, this could result in an organized movement against all management.

Managers must realize that if employees do not receive the respect and recognition they feel is due, they will find other outlets to satisfy this need, and it is usually with each other, collectively.

## Money Motivates People to Show Up

What about money? Money motivates people, doesn't it? Unfortunately, there is no research to validate this belief. In fact, my own studies—which I have been conducting for the past 20 years—show that if you fundamentally believe that money is a primary motivator of higher performance you will *never* become a truly effective iLeader.

Money as a motivator is a myth that many untrained and inexperienced managers believe so they do not have to take responsibility for the unacceptable behaviors and poor performance they are experiencing from their employees. It is much easier to ask human resources and finance to create an incentive program than it is to coach employees using the proper techniques described later in this chapter.

I have personally conducted research with thousands of managers and many more thousands of employees. In all my surveys, managers rank money as one of the top three motivators. Surprisingly, the employees ranked money anywhere from ninth to thirteenth. "Recognition from management" is always in their top three. According to an Indian-based strategy, research, and development firm that interviewed over 1,000 young people, on the top-twelve list of what they want in a dream job, money placed seventh and stock options came in last.

In recent years, I found other interesting rankings. Employees have not only prioritized recognition from management or their relationship with management as their number one motivator; it sometimes receives a score 50% higher than the one in the number two spot. Usually the top five list includes "sufficient responsibility and authority," "meaningful and worthwhile work," and "opportunity for challenging assignments"

Pay is what I call a *show up* factor. It gets people to show up. Once an employee shows up, however, money will not guarantee the quality of their work performance, cause an increase in effectiveness, or inspire creativity. More importantly, it will not develop higher levels of loyalty, create enthusiasm, or ensure ethical work-related behavior.

Elements that contribute to a positive workforce are: providing a suitable, comfortable work environment, a healthy work-life balance, rewarding success and keeping lines of communication between management and staff open. What really gets people of all generations to excel is having a sense of control over their work, their decisions, their time, and their lives.

When organizations enter the black hole of bribing people to perform, it starts a cycle of dependency for empty gratification. As a result, employees will start looking for personal self-fulfillment elsewhere, and they will want even higher salaries just to keep them showing up.

## Recognition from Management as #1 Motivator

My studies have shown that an organization can pay people as much as 20% less than the industry average, and they will stay. This is possible if managers focus on the important areas that really motivate people, e.g., challenging work, opportunity for personal growth, respect from management, real skills being put to use, opportunity to use initiative, and so on.

If the real motivating factors do not exist, however, people may be earning as much as 20% more than the industry average and still quit! Employees would appreciate the boss sincerely saying to them, "Thanks for staying late last night, you really were a big help to us," more than simply giving them 50 bucks.

Managers have told me for years that they believe their younger generation of employees is only motivated by money. I wanted to understand why they think this, because I remember when I started out in the working world, the managers I worked for also thought that money was the only thing that would motivate me. But I knew then it was not true. What people are really looking for is a mix of recognition and challenge — challenge that requires them to stretch, but does not stress them out.

Have you ever wondered why it is that each generation of managers that comes along always believes that money is a primary motivator, even though these same managers say that money is not a motivator for them? In fact, every single piece of research done on motivation over the past 50 years says it just isn't so! There is no evidence that people are motivated to higher levels of performance or increased job satisfaction by bribes of additional compensation or threats of withholding it.

## Four Stages of Motivation

*The ages given in the next illustration are not important, but are used to add context and because they represent a typical pattern for a large segment of our society.*

## Stage One – Achievement

As the graphic on page 106 shows, in the early years of our careers (20 to 35 years of age), our skill level requires a dependency on others, and we go through a phase of uncertainty. The uncertainty exists because we are not sure of our futures. We are not sure of the road to success; we are not even sure if we are in the right occupation. Therefore, we are more focused on work than on people. During this time, we are driven to accumulate wealth and acquire status. This stage is more than just striving for higher earnings; we seek to acquire possessions and firm up a positive self-image

This definition of achievement is primarily determined by our socio-economic status. When our personal perception of wealth and status is more assured and affirmed (which is different for each individual and culture) we will develop greater hope and confidence for the future. This optimism enables us to move to the next stage, where we are more focused, and determined to achieve the success we envisioned early on in life.

## Stage Two – Connection

During this second stage, (which is typically 35 to 50 years of age), we are more motivated to connect with others. In addition to building a stronger professional stature, we also take the time to reach out and connect with other like-minded professionals; develop deeper friendships, become more neighbourly, and reconnect with our immediate and extended families. Now we are equally focused on work as well as people.

## Stage Three – Purpose

Once we have made strong personal connections in our lives, we develop a greater sense of trust and confidence in ourselves and others. This will enable us to move into the next stage, where we feel competent in our work but regress to a feeling of uncertainty about our value and contribution to the world. It is during this third stage (generally between ages 50 and 65) that we ask ourselves, "What is the meaning of my life?" This is the time we develop a strong desire to leave a lasting legacy for the life we have lived. As the old Peggy Lee song says "Is that all there is?"

We are looking for a way to give back and leave the world a better place, or leave our own distinctive legacies. During this time, we may be willing to volunteer and even fight for causes that we feel are just. We give our loyalty to organizations that we perceive are ethical. Our primary motivating factor is to realize a greater purpose. We sense that there must be a deeper reason we were put on the earth other than to work, make money, and enjoy ourselves. At this stage, we generally feel insignificant on a planetary level and want to become spiritually deeper.

## Stage Four – Peace

When we are able to realize our greater purpose – again, this is different for each individual – we come to a place of wisdom and live a life of integrity. This means that what we think will greatly impact how we feel. How we feel is reflected in what we say. And what we say results in what we do. So we consider our thoughts carefully. When we reach this fourth and final stage, we move toward a deepened inner peace, and our whole being is in harmony. Maslow called this highest state of psychological needs "self-actualization." But, as you now understand, it is much more than that.

## Mentoring the Stages of Motivation

iLeaders have an inherent understanding of the four stages of motivation their employees will naturally grow through. Knowing this will give them the ability to create an environment in which all people can feel in control and inspired.

During the first motivational stage, employees constantly assess, at a subconscious level, how decisions enhance or diminish their status. So any stimulus program should be focused on helping bring them closer to enhancing their status and stature in life. It is more than just linear promotions and quarterly performance evaluations; the organization should offer an equitable compensation package with rewards tied to measurable, specific, and timed results.

iLeaders work hard at providing real-time, constructive advice through conversation, often preceded by the question, "May I give you some feedback?" The next step is appropriate praise as well as actionable and constructive advice. Motivation-based coaching will go a long way towards building strong relationships with new workers.

Employees in the second stage of motivation require an environment of relationship building and collaboration. During this phase, people want to spend social, fun time with family and friends, some or many of whom may be their colleagues. Managers must realize this and design work that will support a more balanced life style.

In the third stage, workers want to express their creativity and are less interested in the job. They want to be in a role where they can make a difference. This is a time when some employees may feel their values are diverging from those of their organization. Employees in this stage may appear less dedicated to work or leave the organization if they cannot see the bigger picture of what their job is all about. iLeaders enhance these employees' jobs by putting them in mentoring relationships with more junior employees and encouraging their volunteer or community pursuits, either as individuals or as champions of a cause their organization or team supports.

People in the last stage require a culture of involvement, trust, and constructive communication. iLeaders who have employees in this stage ensure there is an atmosphere of partnership. These employees see themselves as partners in the business and even communicate with clients as if they are. If these employees believe in the mission of their organization and its means and methods of being socially responsible, they will continue to be valuable and highly productive within the organization. They will be the type of people that customers, colleagues, and management call on for the best service or most trusted advice.

Hopefully, this knowledge will help organizations rethink their recognition and retention programs. Although it adds a degree of complexity to the algorithm of management structures, working cultures, and coaching, those that can adapt will be rewarded by retaining more loyal and productive employees. This model shows how people strive to evolve from success to significance.

## Aligning Life Status to Motivation

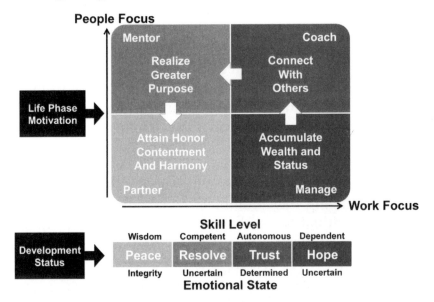

## Aligning Motivation within the Workplace

| Motivator | Thinking | Trigger | Valued For | Environmental Need |
|---|---|---|---|---|
| Accumulate wealth & status | Achievement | Reward & recognition | What you do | Reward tied to results<br>Equitable compensation |
| Connect with others | Affiliative | Collaborative organization culture | Who you know | Value team involvement<br>Encourage sharing<br>Foster relationship building |
| Realize greater purpose | Humanistic | Big picture understanding | Your influence on others | Design roles not jobs<br>Connect roles to vision<br>Allow creative innovation |
| Attain honor, contentment & harmony | Self-actualized | Integration in the ownership | Who you are | Transparent communication<br>Value trust & partnership<br>Culture of involvement |

## Are you "Truly" Motivated?

| SITUATION | RANK (1-10) |
|---|---|

1. How much autonomy do you
   have over your TASKS at work?
   *Your main responsibilities and what you do on
   any given day.*                                    _____

2. How much autonomy do you
   have over your TIME at work?
   *When you arrive, when you leave, and how you
   allocate your hours.*                              _____

3. How much autonomy do you
   have over your TEAM at work?
   *Are you able to choose the people with whom
   you collaborate?*                                  _____

4. How much autonomy do you have
   over your TECHNIQUES at work?
   *The way in which you execute your responsibilities.*   _____

TOTAL*     _____

**\*What is your score? Despondently, a score of 27 or more is good in today's corporate cultural environment.**

## PERSONAL NOTES:

*I will do the following 5 things to improve my motivation:*

1. _____

2. _____

3. _____

4. _____

5. _____

*I would like to put another bold statement here. This is one that will be hard for anyone other than an iLeader to accept. If you want people to increase their quality, effectiveness and productivity – allow afternoon naps.*

### *Allow afternoon naps.*

- Most US Presidents practiced this daily. Lyndon Johnson actually put on his pajamas and got into bed for his nap.

- NASA research shows that pilots' performance improves 34% after a 26-minute nap.

- College studies have shown that student cognitive skills increase over 30% after a nap.

- The *siesta* has been institutionalized in many cultures and countries around the world.

*"One person's commitment to accomplishing
the goal of many is what truly makes a team work."*
- Kristin Arnold

## To Team or Not to Team

There are still many organizations that do not see the benefits of having employees connect and form autonomous teams. We now have many examples of great results, though. When iLeaders create the right environment, provide the proper training, and implement a structure designed to support, they will discover that teams are a superior way to organize work.

An example of a few benefits:

- Teams are more flexible than departments organized in the traditional fashion.

- Employees change their focus from satisfying the needs of higher management to meeting the needs of customers.

- The synergy of connection generates more creative problem solving.

- When the objectives and solutions have been generated by the team, its members feel more commitment and accountability.

- When people connect in a team, they build on each other's skills.

- Teams improve the bottom line.

There will be executives who question this last point and ask how teams improve the bottom line. Here are a few reasons:

- Teams reduce the need for ongoing supervision. This results in less front-line managers and bureaucracy.
- Teams are more focused on serving customers' needs than meeting internal requirements of the organization.
- Teams implement decisions more effectively if they are not top-down directed.
- People connected in a team structure have higher morale.

**The quality of any solution is directly proportional to the amount of information put on the table to create that solution.**

### Stages of High-Performing Teams

Teams experience different stages of group development on their journey to high performance, and individuals behave differently in different stages. The stages are known as *forming, storming, norming* and *performing.* These four stages, as made popular by Bruce Tuckman in the 1960s, are very predictable, and no group can escape the journey.

The Forming-Storming-Norming-Performing theory is an elegant and helpful explanation of team development and behavior. Other models offer a similar structure, such as the Tannenbaum and Schmidt Continuum or Hersey and Blanchard's Situational Leadership® model, developed about the same time.

Tuckman's model explains that as the team develops maturity and ability, relationships are established, and the leader changes leadership style

### Forming

In the 'forming' stage, the members usually feel some excitement and eagerness at the promise of a new working environment. The expectations are high, and everyone is looking forward to great success. Although there may be some anxiety about what is going on, the productivity and efficiency of the team increases regularly.

If the team is in the forming stage the leader must recognize that members will have a high need for structure and certainty. The best thing the leader can do is provide an overall orientation, articulate the vision, and create a clear framework within which the group must operate, provide a comfortable non-judgmental environment, clarify why each member is on the team, and help individuals clarify their personal goals.

### Storming

At some point after the formation has taken place, teams will "storm." Although this stage cannot be avoided, if the leader did everything correctly in the forming stage (most don't) the storming can be mitigated so the next stage can be reached more quickly, without a substantial loss in productivity and efficiency. If not handled properly, the storming could go on for months and even cause the disintegration of the team.

One trigger for this stage is that people experience disappointment because their initial hopes for the team aren't realized. They might storm about the volume of work, tight time schedules, or the frustration of long meetings. They might also storm against each other. They form cliques, or members find themselves at cross-purposes.

Usually the storming causes a reaction against the leader, who has the most power and is the most convenient person to blame for the team's problems. Some members may even start having private meetings and not invite the leader.

This is the toughest stage, and it often causes the senior management to disband the team and decide that self-managed teams may be good in concept but don't really work. Leaders must remember that this is a natural part of a team's development, and they must respond to the storming with the right strategies to get through this stage constructively.

The main role of the leader in this stage is to understand that the team needs to "air" differences and deal with conflict. I will go into greater detail on this subject in the chapter on Conflict. The worst thing to do at this time is to suppress conflict and ask people to start getting along. The leader must take on a facilitator role, stay neutral, not react emotionally, and create a constructive problem-solving process and environment.

When I work with teams I use non-threatening simulation exercises for members to develop and practice problem-solving skills. I also employ the use of 360° feedback instruments so team members can better understand how their behaviors and styles are affecting the response of others with whom they must work.

## Norming

The next stage, "norming," will come more quickly if the leader is able to effectively deal with the issues in the storming stage and create an environment of learning and developing. Norming is the stage where the team, along with management, will articulate expectations, the degree of empowerment is defined, and boundaries are explained. This is also when the organization implements education and training programs and the team agrees on a code of conduct for working together becomes documented.

When this happens the team members will experience an increasing level of satisfaction because they have solved some major problems and resolved personal conflicts. They will conduct themselves by the new rules of engagement.

During this stage, an iLeader will start relinquishing control over how to achieve team goals to members. An important part of the norming stage is training. However, it must be very pragmatic, skills-based training including topics like conflict management, thinking styles, decision making styles and process agreement strategies. It should not be the training many receive where they end with a group hug singing *Kumbaya*.

## Performing

If the iLeader has handled the three phases correctly and the team is now working together, they will go into the fourth stage, called "performing." At this stage, the team is ready to settle down and get to the real work at hand. People become more excited as they see progress, and feel positive because they are working collaboratively.

Members know each other's skills, are sensitive to each other's needs, have co-dependent or symbiotic relationships and have high confidence in their ability to accomplish their objectives.

The leader must be very careful not to dominate, take back control, or take personal credit for the team's accomplishments. They must put in place a system of rewards not only for positive results, but also for team behaviors, which are conducive to a constructive working environment.

Getting to this stage is hard work, and attempting a shortcut will only result in regression. Team members will become cynical and resist getting back together.

## Other Stages

If the stages are navigated correctly, however, there will be a more collegial environment between the leader and the team. In fact, if the leader has done a really good job in connecting the team, they will be able to stop being a leader all the time, and the role becomes shared by the various members on certain projects.

In the recent past, thousands of innovative and responsive organizations learned about the importance of shifting decision-making to the lowest possible level in the organization. But that shift cannot happen overnight, and cannot be implemented simply by hanging inspirational posters on the walls and bringing the employees together for a free coffee and T-shirt.

The good news is that connecting and empowering employees is not a vague concept based on a trial and error process.

*There is a very concrete formula for sorting out the specific degrees of empowerment for different levels within organizations and developing a strategy to enable them to get to a position of positive performance.*

### Selecting the Team

In order to be a team player, you have to think and behave like a team player.

To create a constructive working relationship, achieve harmony in the workplace, and reduce conflict, there are two key players in the process. One, of course, is the individual, and the other is the individual's manager.

I will deal with the manager's role and its influence on an employee's behavior in the chapter on Coaching. In this chapter, I will focus on the way past experiences and current environment influence people's thoughts and behavior. It is a person's own mental conditioning and environment that determine their style of thinking. This thinking style will then translate into either appropriate or inappropriate behavior. People have to ask themselves: "Who am I?" and "What causes me to act the way I do?" The answers to these questions are the key to career success, effective leadership, and avoiding conflict in life.

In his book *Manifest Your Destiny*, Dr. Wayne W. Dyer uses the analogy that if you squeeze an orange, you will get orange juice. If your boss squeezes an orange, he will get orange juice. If your spouse squeezes an orange, she will also get orange juice. Why? Because that what is in an orange. It does not matter who puts pressure on it; orange juice is what will come out.

People are the same way. What is in you – is in you, and it does not matter who squeezes (puts pressure) on you. Whatever is in you will come out. It does not matter who squeezes us, whether it is our spouse, our boss, or life in general. However, there is a difference – we can choose what is in us and change the way we respond when we are squeezed. But first we must know what is currently in us and why it is there, and then take action to change.

We are all aware that every hour of every day of every week we are bombarded with stimuli. They may come in the form of an event, a situation, or an encounter with another person. We have all been conditioned to respond in a way that we feel is right. This response can either be appropriate or inappropriate.

The reason individuals respond differently is directly related to how they think of that event, situation, or person. This will result in them behaving either passively, aggressively, or constructively.

### Conditioned, Reactive Thinking

Let me give you an example. You are driving down the highway, listening to the radio, minding your own business, and going the speed limit. Suddenly, a red sports car with tinted windows and a loud engine squeezes by you, causing you to almost go off the road, then forces its way in front of you. How do you feel? What do you do? What happens to you physiologically? Physically, if you are like many people, your heart races, your blood pressure goes up, and your gastro-intestinal system increases its secretion of acids. Behaviorally, you might ride up on the sports car's bumper, blast your horn, and try to pass him, or give him the finger.

Others might instead say, "Oh my!" and nearly drive into the ditch to get out of the sports car's way, back off, perhaps even causing someone else to go off the road, and then feel all shook up over the event. Still others might carefully slow down to avoid an accident, consider that they may have been in the sports car's blind spot, or even believe there might be some legitimate reason the driver of that red sports car did what he did.

Let me tell the story again with a new detail. You are driving down the highway, listening to the radio, going the speed limit, and minding your own business. The radio announcer interrupts the music and says, "Folks, if you happen to be driving down this particular highway, there is a young man in a red sports car rushing to the hospital. His wife is in the back seat and she is in labor; he is trying to get her to the hospital as quickly as..." Suddenly, a red sports car with tinted windows and a loud engine squeezes by you, causing you to almost go off the road, and forces its way in front of you.

How do you feel? What do you do? What happens to you physiologically? How did you feel when you arrived at work, or at home and encountered a co-worker or spouse wanting your attention? Probably, your heart rate and blood pressure would not go up much, nor would your stomach be upset. You would probably act appropriately on the highway and drive around the situation carefully. When you arrived at home or work and encountered a co-worker or spouse your mood would probably be more positive.

Why did you behave differently in each of those situations? Many people will answer, "The situation changed." However, it did not. Both situations were exactly the same. The only thing that changed was what you thought of the driver of the sports car. You behaved differently because the radio announcer gave you additional information, causing you to think differently.

We all have to be conscious of the fact that our behavior is based on what we think. And who really is responsible for putting information into our heads? We are. We are responsible for how we think and therefore we must filter and interpret information differently to enable us to behave more appropriately.

Often people say to me, "Well what if the driver in the sports car is really just a jerk?" Well, the answer is, "So what?" You are changing your thinking for *you*, not for that driver.

This little story illustrates that how you think about or interpret situations will have long-term effects on your health, relationships, and what success you might reach in your career.

> **What others say or do is their stuff. How we react to what others say or do is our stuff.**

In order to be successful as an iLeader, you must think in positive ways and behave constructively. It is also important that members of the team also think and behave constructively. But how can you tell whether they do? More importantly, how can you tell how they will behave when under pressure — especially before they are even on the team? I use the LSI Stylus™, created by Human

Synergistics®. This 360° feedback tool, which has been around for many years and has an extremely high validation, analyzes and measures an individual's attitude and behavior against the following styles.

## The Four Constructive Styles:

**Achievement**    A way of thinking that develops effectiveness by setting specific, measurable goals and working towards them with unbending determination.

**Self-Actualizing**    A way of thinking that results in the highest form of personal fulfillment through a high acceptance of self.

**Humanistic**    Personal interest in other people and desire to help others improve.

**Affiliative**    Commitment to forming and sustaining satisfying relationships.

## The Four Passive-Defensive Styles:

**Approval**    A need to be accepted by others to increase one's self-worth. Those seeking approval typically try to please everyone but themselves.

**Conventional**    Tendency to act in a conforming way. Conventional people focus on following rules simply for the sake of following rules.

**Dependent**    Belief that personal efforts do not matter. This manifests itself in a high need for security and self-protection. These people believe that their opinion does not matter, and they cannot influence their future or life.

**Avoidance**    These people have a tendency to withdraw in a confrontational situation. Avoidant people hide their feelings and shy away from situations they find threatening.

## The Four Aggressive-Defensive Styles:

**Oppositional** Oppositional people often disagree with others and seek attention by being cynical and critical.

**Power** The association of self-worth with one's ability to control others.

**Competitiveness** The need to establish a sense of self-worth by competing against and comparing oneself to others.

**Perfectionistic** A driving need to be seen by others as perfect and to avoid mistakes. But the attitude of perfectionism and the act of striving for perfection should not be confused. They are dramatically different.

Here is an example of a more dysfunctional profile as measured by the Human Synergistics® Stylus report. The Constructive styles are arranged from the 11 o'clock position to the 2 o'clock position. The Passive styles are from 3 to 6 o'clock, and the Aggressive styles are from 7 to 10.

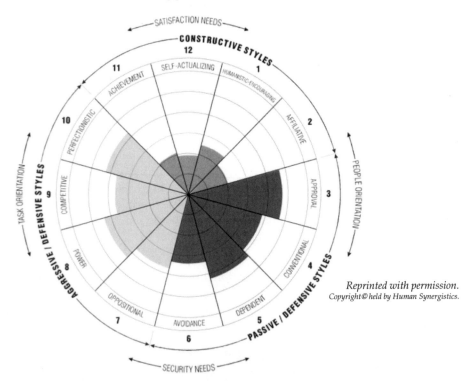

*Reprinted with permission.*
*Copyright© held by Human Synergistics.*

Notice the low scores on the Constructive styles and the proportionally higher ones in the Passive-Defensive and Aggressive styles.

People whose profiles have low scores in the constructive category do not document or focus on goals and do not believe that an individual can make a difference. They will try to blame others for their own personal failure and might shy away from challenging tasks. Those with low scores in Self-Actualization are not committed to the organization, do not accept change easily, and become defensive and depressed when out of their comfort zones. People with low scores in the Humanistic category do not care about the growth and development in others and tend to focus on themselves. They avoid even healthy conflicts and are not interested in serving as a role model for others. People who score low in the Affiliative category are not friendly or cooperative towards others, and do not accept change readily.

In the Passive-Defensive styles, people with a high score in Approval support those with the most authority, try to agree with everyone, and set goals that please others. Those with high scores in the Conventional category treat rules as more important than ideas and people, and follow policies and practices by the book. People who have high scores in the Dependent style rely on others for direction, are good followers, and do not challenge others. People with high scores in Avoidance personalities "lay low" when things get tough, avoid conflict, and struggle over most decisions.

In the Aggressive-Defensive styles, people who score high in the Oppositional category oppose new ideas, look for others' mistakes, and resist change. People with high Power scores want to control everything. They believe in using force to get what they want, seldom admit to their own mistakes, and have very little confidence in other people. Those with high scores in the Competitive style have a strong need to "win" and are the kind of people who compete rather than cooperate. They constantly compare themselves to others. Perfectionists never want to make mistakes, set unrealistic goals, try to take care of every detail personally, and create stress.

A more functional profile, one with higher scores on the Constructive styles and lower scores on both the Aggressive and Passive styles would look similar to the following figure.

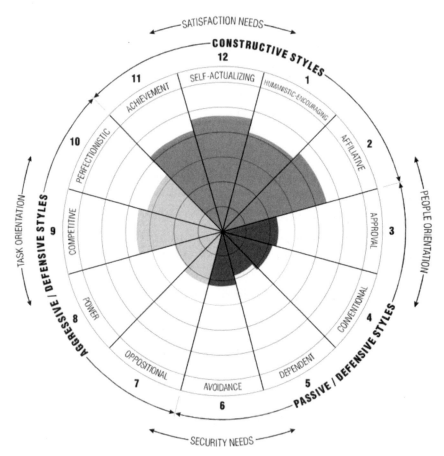

*Reprinted with permission. Copyright© held by Human Synergistics.*

People with a profile like this would display more positive attitudes and behaviors, represented by appropriate scores in each of the three categories.

People with ideal Constructive profiles who score high in Achievement anticipate future trends and opportunities, take reasonable and well-calculated risks, and take initiative to get things done. They try to select team members that will complement the skills of others.

Self-Actualized people deal with issues objectively and honestly, and stand up for what they believe. They generate unique solutions to problems.

Humanistic individuals are sensitive to the needs of others, encourage others to express their ideas, and promote openness. They motivate others by serving as role models.

Affiliative people gain cooperation through personal loyalties. They are charismatic and share personal feelings easily.

People who have appropriately moderate scores in the Approval category are friendly, accept others' values, and rely on their own judgment. People with low scores in the Conventional category are not bound by policy and are able to bend the rules when necessary, though they are tactful when appropriate. They are not upset by change. Those with low Dependent scores do not depend on others for ideas; they like responsibility and are capable of taking charge. People with low Avoidance scores do not procrastinate, are proactive in problem solving, and are willing to take risks.

Ideal Aggressive styles include a low score in the Oppositional category. Such people question decisions made by others and have an ability to ask tough, probing questions. People who have a low score in Power respect the chain of command, are interested in gaining influence, and expect loyalty from their people. Those with low scores in the Competitive category are persistent, self-assertive, and realistic about their accomplishments. People with an appropriately moderate score in Perfectionistic will work to obtain quality results, and have an efficient, business-like approach to tasks. They do not jeopardize the completion of tasks by demanding exact perfection.

I now have many clients who do not hire anyone for professional positions without conducting a simple paper-based form of LSI Stylus™.[4] I even have clients who ask me to do a complete 360° analysis of any candidate for promotion into a senior management position. Organizations that follow this practice have been able to decrease their attrition rate significantly and enjoy effective teams who work together in positive harmony.

## A Word of Caution about Assessment Tools

No single assessment tool is comprehensive enough to capture the richness of a person. The full range of emotions, desires, thoughts, and potential can only be described by the individuals themselves. And yet, I have seen people confuse an assessment model with the person.

Some people identify themselves as a certain type as if they are always and forever fixed. They ignore the fact that these assessment tools are only meant to reveal tendencies and preferences, and that the outcome can and will be influenced by external factors. They lose sight of their own uniqueness and their potential to change.

---

[4] *LSI (Life Styles Inventory)™ All rights reserved by Human Synergistics Canada®. If you would like to complete an LSI™, email info@ethos.ca*

As stated by James Flaherty, author of the insightful book *Coaching: Evoking Excellence in Others*: "Human beings in every case will exist beyond the borders of whatever model is used to describe them; that a model is at best a well-focused snapshot; and that human beings are living, changing, adapting, and self-interpreting."

There is a danger that assessment tools can lead to creating a Pygmalion Effect, or self-fulfilling prophecy. If a person accepts the instrument to be an inflexible assessment of who they are, what they prefer, and how they behave, they may accept this label and only see themselves within the narrow confines of the assessment model. We all know the hazard of being labeled by someone.

The power of a teacher on a young person's life has been well-documented. If a teacher believes a child is a low performer and treats that child according to that label, the child will often come to believe that they are a low performer and behave accordingly, even though they may be very bright.

How often have you heard people label themselves? Labels like: "I'm not smart enough," "I'm just a shy person," or "I don't have the talent to do that."

*"Self-assessment is essential for progress as a learner:*
*For understanding of selves as learners, for an increasingly*
*complex understanding of tasks and learning goals,*
*and for strategic knowledge of how*
*to go about improving."*

- D.R. Sadler

# iLeader Profile

## *Elaine Gutmacher*

*Elaine Gutmacher is the Director of Operations for the Schulich Executive Education Centre (SEEC) at the Schulich School of Business of York University. She is an amazing people person, team builder, and always focused on ensuring that her team is working collaboratively.*

E laine Gutmacher has climbed the ladder of success from a Secretary to the Director of Operations of SEEC, and her accomplishments have positively affected thousands of business managers and professionals all around the globe.

In our interview, Elaine spoke of the great mentors and people who believed in her—sometimes more than she believed in herself. Some of those mentors include Elmer Phillips, Peter Zarry, and Alan Middleton. But it is from her father, a successful entrepreneur and businessman, that she learned the entrepreneurial spirit, her work ethic, and the value of treating people well.

She learned early on that little can be accomplished without a talented and supportive team who feel valued for their contribution. She has had very little turnover through the years, and her people respect her highly. Her day-to-day focus is to create a culture of community in the workplace. She holds regular town hall meetings to ensure everyone is aware of any new strategies or changes.

One reason she stands out from other managers is her value of "fairness": fairness to her staff, fairness to her suppliers, and fairness to her clients. Every decision she makes is made on the foundation of fairness to all stakeholders.

As with many of the great and successful people I work with and have interviewed, Elaine did not start in business with a high level of academic achievement. If she could change one thing, it would be to have furthered her education. Not that it would have improved how she actually performed at work — in fact, she has consistently outperformed her peers who have higher academic credentials — but it would have opened more doors to her initially. Nevertheless, her street smarts, experience, and ability to make clear decisions even when the choices are fuzzy have more than compensated for any benefit a higher education might have afforded.

Her people management focus is to treat each individual with consideration, courtesy, and kindness; to be clear on expectations; to give rewards appropriately and in a timely manner; and to provide on-going, regular feedback. In an environment with very little flexibility to use money or other benefits as a motivator, she considers all aspects of an employee's intrinsic needs.

She feels that one of today's biggest business challenges is the movement towards electronic communication. She makes sure there is lots of face-to-face time with her staff and deals promptly with any elephants in the room. She encourages everyone to be open and candid yet respectful.

The key to her overall success is her belief that "Failure is just not an option." No matter what challenge she has faced, she only focused on: "How can I make this work," rather than dwelling on the reasons why it could not.

Elaine Gutmacher started her career with the Schulich Executive Education Centre (SEEC) formally known as the Division of Executive Development, as Secretary to the Director. She was quickly promoted to Administrative Assistant and then to Administrative Officer.

In 1997 she left York University to become President of her own printing franchise, which she ran successfully for eight years. In 1994, at the request of the Dean of Schulich, Elaine took a three-month leave of absence from her business to return to SEEC to reorganize the division due to the phenomenal growth that SEEC was experiencing. During that time, her husband Sam, who owned his own printing franchise, took over the running of Elaine's business as well.

The Dean asked Elaine to stay on as Assistant Director after the reorganization. She amalgamated the two printing franchises into one location and returned to SEEC on a full-time basis. In the fall of 2000, she was promoted to Associate Director, Operations and in 2006 she was promoted to Director of Operations.

Elaine is responsible for the open enrollment programs, the centers of Excellence, and the University Partnership Program, and is the HR Prime. Elaine has been instrumental in the growth of the SEEC, from training around 1,000 managers per year to almost 20,000 managers per year nationally and internationally.

# Summary
## *Chapter Two*

## Workers of the Future

- 🌀 *Traditionalists 1920 – 1945.*
- 🌀 *Baby Boomers 1946 – 1964.*
- 🌀 *Generation "X" 1965 – 1979.*
- 🌀 *Generation "Y" 1980 – 1990.*
- 🌀 *Millennial Generation 1991 – present.*

## A Very Special Workforce

- 🌀 *Understanding Millennials.*
- 🌀 *Inspiring the Boomers.*
- 🌀 *General motivation.*
- 🌀 *Employment trends research.*

## A Quilting Bee Concept for Teams

- 🌀 *An effective working culture.*
- 🌀 *Our conditioned behaviors.*
- 🌀 *Prisoners of our paradigms.*
- 🌀 *The monkey's dilemma.*

## Motivation & Behavior

- 🌀 *Factors of intrinsic motivation.*
- 🌀 *Evolution of motivation.*
- 🌀 *Sherren's Hierarchy of Motivation©.*
- 🌀 *Constructive, Aggressive or Passive behaviors.*

# Chapter Three

## Coaching the Employees

*"Encourage and reinforce human performance."*

I am going to start this chapter with another bold statement. I believe that in today's environment, the typical annual performance review process now being used in most organizations is just not working. It is an outdated and painful process for both the manager and the employee, and does not add any value to increasing the motivation, loyalty, or productivity of most employees. In fact, as Hertzberg might say, it is probably more of a *de-motivator*. It is really just a modern day version of bullying and intimidation in a modern, socially acceptable format.

## Scrap the Annual Performance Review

When first implemented back in the 1960s it was an attempt to bring fairness into the "pay for performance" culture. Before that, there was a fair compensation process known as "piece work." If you built 10 widgets you would get paid for 10. If you built 15, then you would be paid accordingly. This was fair. So, in the absence of a process like this for the more professional or clerical jobs, the Performance Appraisal system was an attempt to bring about an equitable and objective way of dispensing compensation that would also appear fair to employees.

Today, it is one of the leftover relics of the Bureaucratic Stage. It has become a costly, make-work program for managers and human resources specialists, and the time has come to scrap this subjective, outdated, de-motivating practice.

*The current Performance Appraisal Process is just a modernized and legitimate form of bullying and intimidation, resulting in a make-work program for the HR department.*

This outdated process runs the risk of destroying otherwise good relationships between managers and employees.

If anyone reading this disagrees, please think this scenario through. Do you volunteer for any organization? Are you intrinsically motivated to do that? Do you enjoy the time you spend volunteering? Think about why you replied "yes" to these questions.

What if I said to you, "From now on, in recognition for your great volunteering efforts, I am going to pay you $10.00

an hour. I know that's not much, but it's a lot more than you're getting now. Then, at the end of every year, just to help you improve your motivation towards volunteering and inspire you to do higher quality volunteering, I am going to give you a performance review and rate you on a scale against your peers." Would you be more motivated? Or would you just quit volunteering?

Here is one alternative appraisal system. What if every year (or two) your customers, your co-workers, and your boss (together) were able to vote on whether or not you could keep your job? Did you add value in the form of increased revenue or decreased costs? Did you contribute to a more collaborative environment? Did you increase customer satisfaction? What behaviors might that system translate into? Let's stop worrying about trying to fit all employees into the old, convenient bell-curve skew of performance, which in many organizations is very subjective anyway.

Here is an even better idea. What if everyone you hire is placed on an employment contract that has an expiry of two, three, or five years (depending on the level and complexity of the job)? That way, at the expiry, ether party could walk away with no obligations. At the end of this period, the employee would have to re-apply for his or her job and the employer would have to convince the employee to stay. I bet it would certainly change the behavior of both the employee and the manager.

### iLeaders Manage People Like They are all Volunteers

Perhaps leaders would then begin to manage their people like *they were all volunteers*. And employees would ensure that they were continually adding value to the organization and focus on building and maintaining positive relationships with management and other staff.

*Managers should work like they own the organization and manage their people like they are all volunteers*

## iLeaders are Great Coaches

Please do not do something as radical as scrapping the annual performance review process immediately, and without alternatives, although I do believe the time for significant change is close. In many professions, such as entertainment or sports, you either get to keep your job or not as a consequence of performance. People in my business are evaluated at the end of every speech, every event, and every day. It is decided right then whether we will be asked back to that audience or organization or not.

Not that I hold it up as the ideal structure, but even our politicians have to prove their value to their customers every four years. Their customers vote on whether they can keep their jobs, and some end up losing their positions. This system is sometimes flawed since there are other, more complex issues involved in that profession — *like politics*. In addition, politicians are able to influence their customers (voters) by bribing them with their own money.

Instead of making a dramatic change like that just yet, why don't we create a culture of continuing, constructive coaching? That way, employees know instantly, daily, or weekly how they are doing. This would enable them to either take corrective action immediately or realize there is a bad fit with the work or the company culture. If they are unable to improve their performance or behavior, then the manager could take steps right away to resolve the mismatch between employee skills and job requirements.

- A good Leader knows the right road to take.
- A good Manager will ensure the right people are going down the road efficiently.
- A good Coach will help people stay focused, positive, and navigate the road ahead.

## Does Coaching Work?

The process of coaching is the most important intervention a manager can have with an employee. Some of the reasons coaching must be practiced are:

- To integrate a new employees into the organization.
- To prepare people to adapt to change.
- To help employees deal with personal and business issues.
- To mentor employees so that they achieve their career goals.
- To ensure employees provide ROI by improving performance.
- To inspire employees to do their best.
- To create a long-term loyalty to their profession and organization.

- To align employees' goals with the mission of the organization.

Effective coaching contributes to an organization's bottom line. Proper coaching results in highly competent, productive, and constructive employees. It also reduces turnover, and is one of the major contributing factors in keeping talented people. Incorrect coaching results in employees acting either passive or aggressive, and inhibits their personal development and potential.

*"Coaching is a way of working with people that leaves them more competent and more fulfilled so that they are more able to contribute to their organizations and find meaning in what they are doing."*

- James Flaherty

## What Are Your Coaching Strengths?

*Please read each question and circle the letter indicating the action you would choose under those circumstances:*

1. An important change in procedures is now required. All your employees have a consistent fine record of accomplishment. They have experience and continue to work well together. They also realize this change is necessary.

   a) *Allow the team to participate with you in developing the change. Explain the reasons for the change, but try not to be too directive.*

   b) *State the changes and then implement them with close supervision.*

   c) *Let the team develop and implement their own recommendations.*

   d) *Incorporate the team's recommendations, but maintain control.*

2. Lately, the results being achieved by an employee who you felt had potential have been dropping. He seems unconcerned about meeting objectives. He continually needs follow-up to ensure the task is done correctly and on time. There are no issues of a personal nature.

   a) *Let the employee formulate his own direction.*

   b) *Incorporate the employee's recommendations, but explain performance requirements and see that his objectives are met.*

   c) *Review his role and responsibilities then supervise closely.*

   d) *Allow his involvement in determining his roles and responsibilities. Listen to his suggestions and don't be too directive.*

3. You are a new manager in an efficiently run organization. The previous manager tightly controlled and directed the team. You want to maintain this productive situation, but would like to begin humanizing the environment and building relationships.

   a) *Do what you can to make the team feel important and involved.*

   b) *Continue to supervise carefully and emphasize the importance of deadlines and tasks.*

   c) *Since you are new, intentionally avoid intervention.*

   d) *Encourage the team's involvement in decision-making but ensure objectives are met by explaining performance requirements.*

4. You are considering changing to a structure that will be new to your employee. Although she is apprehensive about proceeding, she has made suggestions about the needed change. This employee has been productive and demonstrated knowledge, experience, and skills in executing her responsibilities.

   a) *Define specifically the change and direct its implementation.*

   b) *Encourage her to develop the change process and ask her how she might organize the implementation.*

   c) *Be willing to make changes as recommended, but maintain control and responsibility for the implementation.*

   d) *She has a good record; leave things alone.*

**Correct answers will be discussed later in this chapter.**

## Pillars of Competency

In my training sessions, I ask managers, "If you have a high-potential employee who is deserving of a promotion or higher responsibility, what are some words you would use to describe him or her?" As they shout out the words, I put them in two columns as follows:

| (A) | (B) |
|---|---|
| Experienced | Self-Motivated |
| Educated | Enthusiastic |
| Shows Judgment | Cooperative |
| Trained | Committed |
| Innovative | Flexible |
| Proven Track Record | Self-Confident |

The (A) column I describe as those items that give the employee the ability to do the job, while the (B) column represents those attributes that give the employee the eagerness to do the job. I then ask over which column the audience thinks a manager has more direct control. Invariably, I get "A" as their answer. Actually, as managers, they have the ability to influence both columns equally. I call these the pillars of competency. If someone were to score high marks on both of these columns, you would consider them highly competent and would like them working for you. But, if they scored very low marks on each of these pillars, you would not consider them very competent and you would prefer not to have them working for you.

***The main purpose of coaching is to enable ordinary employees to achieve extraordinary things.***

### Focusing on Strengths

Some managers seem to have a more natural ability to build healthy coaching relationships. They are sensitive to their employees' needs and focus on what employees do well in order to help them perform even better. Other managers are more concerned about their personal agendas and focus on the negative aspects and what their employees do wrong.

As I said earlier in our introduction, my goal with this book, my speeches, and workshops is to help create a healthy workplace where people are doing what they love to do in an environment that supports and encourages the development of their strengths.

We have all heard many times from many pieces of research that the number one reason most people leave their jobs is because of their manager, or not feeling appreciated.

In fact, according to Tom Rath and Donald O. Clifton, authors of *How Full Is Your Bucket? Positive Strategies for Work and Life,* 65% of people surveyed said they received no recognition for good work at their jobs.

In 2005, Jerry Krueger and Emily Killham shared the results of Gallup research, which revealed that what employees want most (along with competitive pay) is quality management. When they feel unappreciated and disapprove of their managers, they leave or join the growing ranks of the disengaged.

## Creating Positive Leadership

Managers play a crucial role in employee well being and engagement — but what can they do to elicit positive responses?

Margaret Greenberg and Dana Arakawa, both graduates of the Master of Applied Positive Psychology program at the University of Pennsylvania, put the theory of positive leadership to the test. They wanted to know if managers who apply positive leadership practices have teams with higher project performance and employee engagement.

As it turns out, positive managers practice three leadership behaviors:

1. Use a strengths-based approach.
2. Provide frequent recognition and encouragement.
3. Maintain a positive perspective when difficulties arise

None of these are innate behaviors, but all can be learned.

## Focusing on weaknesses is a paternalistic practice

Unfortunately, most organizations are obsessed with fixing weaknesses. They conduct performance reviews, 360-degree assessments, and the like, to evaluate how well employees and managers are measuring up to predefined goals and competencies.

Managers are instructed to look at an employee's assessment and coach for greater performance in areas of weakness. But such assessments usually pay only cursory attention to an employee's strengths. Performance reviews and subsequent remedial programs focus almost exclusively on weaknesses.

What organizations should be focusing on is creating a strengths-based approach that involves helping managers become more positive and supportive coaches. In my experience, this process becomes easier when the manager is able to focus on the employees' strengths while coaching them to manage their weaknesses. There is a parable, which has been around for many years, about animals who decided to start a school. The story goes like this:

## The Animal School

*Once upon a time, the animals decided they must do something heroic to overcome the problems of "a new world." So they organized a school.*

*They adopted an activity curriculum consisting of running, climbing, swimming, and flying. To make it easier to administer the curriculum, all the animals took all the subjects.*

*The duck was excellent in swimming, in fact better than his instructor, but he made only passing grades in flying and was very poor in running. Since he was slow in running, he had to stay after school and also drop swimming in order to practice running. This was kept up until his webbed feet were badly worn and he became only average in swimming. But average was acceptable in school, so nobody worried about that except the duck.*

*The rabbit started at the top of the class in running, but had a nervous breakdown because of so much make-up work in swimming.*

*The squirrel was excellent in climbing until he developed frustration in the flying class, where his teacher made him start from the ground up instead of from the treetop down. He also developed a "charley horse" from overexertion and got a "C" in climbing and a "D" in running.*

*The eagle was a problem child and was disciplined severely. In the climbing class, he beat all the others to the top of the tree, but insisted on using his own way to get there.*

*At the end of the year, an abnormal eel, who could swim exceedingly well, run, climb, and fly a little, had the highest average and was valedictorian.*

*The prairie dogs stayed out of the school and fought the tax levy because the administration would not add digging and burrowing to the curriculum. They apprenticed their children to a badger and later joined the groundhogs and gophers to start a successful private school.*

The moral of this story is that too often you are told you are not good enough unless you change. And change, in this case, means working on your weaknesses. Managers may suggest that you undergo remedial training in order to overcome your weaknesses, or just tell you to work harder. Unfortunately, if you are focused only on weaknesses, you will waste a lot of energy and negate your strengths. Focusing on the failures in your work will only make you feel worse, and you will inevitably neglect the successes.

The greatest chance for creating a healthy coaching relationship with your employees lies in remembering and improving the good things, and getting back on track while doing fewer bad things. Just like Donald O. Clifton and Paula Nelson suggest in *Soar With Your Strengths*, "If you develop your strengths to the maximum, the strength becomes so great it overwhelms the weaknesses."

*Instead of working on what is wrong with a person, identify and develop what is right.*

## The Constructive Coach

Think about what coaching would be like if managers devoted more time to discovering what their employees appreciate and enjoy. Imagine spending most of your time working on strengths until the positive experiences simply overwhelm the negative ones.

You may have heard the story about the Swedish table tennis player Jan-Ove Waldner who spent much of his time training in China. It seems this particular player had a major weakness. He couldn't produce a backhand stroke; he only used forehand strokes. His competition knew this, so the coaches instructed all their players to go for his backhand. "Get the ball there and you've got him beat. He won't be able to return it!" they said. So they did. Player after player won a point whenever they shot the ball at his backhand.

Unfortunately for them, they just couldn't get the ball to his backhand often enough to make a difference. Jan-Ove won the gold medal. You see, he was playing with his strength. When the coach of the Chinese team was interviewed and asked about his training method, he replied, "We practice eight hours a day perfecting our strengths." He instinctively knew that if his player's strong forehand became even stronger, it would overwhelm his weak backhand.

Imagine what coaching would be like if you came in and started talking about what was right with your work, and you just wanted to learn how to make it even better.

The answer lies in encouraging and reinforcing those things the people do best, while coaching them to manage the things they don't do well.

### *iLeaders who are extraordinary coaches focus on and develop each individual's strengths.*

Coaches should be wary of the phrase, "Let me show you how," when coaching a team member through a new task. When you're in a rush, it's tempting to demonstrate a task rather than to provide supportive direction. The real motivation behind "Let me show you how" is usually to get the work done and look like a hero rather than to help the team member develop.

This may boost short-term performance, but long-term effectiveness suffers. Before you demonstrate a task, ask yourself:

1.  Am I supporting the team member or helping myself?

2.  Will my actions increase or decrease employee independence?

## Heroes Are Not Welcome

There is a "factorial system" of management currently operating in most North American organizations. It is also referred to as the "Hero Management Style". It goes like this: The manager is the one who sets direction, answers questions, makes the tough decisions, and shoulders most of the responsibility. In short, the manager rides in on a white horse and acts like a hero to save the day. And yet, I find that in many organizations, when a hero is needed, the hero caused the crisis in the first place.

Have you ever worked at an organization that underwent a crisis on either a daily or weekly basis? In these situations, the manager typically brings everyone together at lunch, buys pizza, and everyone stays overtime to solve the crisis. This continues to happen regularly, until the manager goes away on a business trip or vacation for a few weeks. Surprisingly, there are no crises. But, the day after the manager returns, all of a sudden there is a crisis.

This syndrome has a name, *Münchausen syndrome by proxy*, borrowed from the medical condition where the affected person actually causes another person — usually his or her child — injury in order to gain attention from the medical profession, family, and friends. Would you believe, there are managers who do just that. They actually cause crises in their organization just so they can look like a hero by solving them—then take all the credit. At a conscious level, however, they do not know they are doing this. It is all happening at a sub-conscious level, so it is useless to try and point this out to them.

*Münchausen syndrome by proxy* in the workplace is another behavior that has come out of the factories of the industrial age. The word *factory* is derived from an East Indian word *factor*, meaning "agents from another land."

It developed during a time when the British ruled India and forced the populace to work under oppressive conditions. The system was highly efficient and regarded as the finest example of bureaucracy. Now the factorial model of leadership is conditioned deeply into our culture and psyche. Even when well-meaning employees say, "I will never be like my manager," they often end up behaving exactly the same way.

Using the factorial model, executives operate under the following assumptions:

- The manager's opinion is always right.
- Managers must have their people "under control."
- Mangers must know what is going on all the time.
- Managers should have better technical expertise than those they lead.
- Managers are responsible for solving all problems.
- Managers are fully responsible for results.

An interesting transformation takes place when an individual is promoted to management. The new manager takes on the behaviors they associate with that role, often just mimicking managers from the early working years.

I am reminded of the scene in "One Flew Over the Cuckoo's Nest" starring Jack Nicholson. In the mental hospital where Nicholson's character R.P. McMurphy was confined, all the patients walked with a slump, dragged their feet and had sullen looks on their faces. However, when McMurphy stole some uniforms for them to wear, the patients immediately stood up straight, put on looks of determination, and walked with purpose. When they were caught and had to put their patient clothes back on, they immediately reverted to their sullen looks, walking with a limp and losing all facial expression. This is because the roles of doctors and nurses and the roles of patients were programmed into their minds, and they conformed to those roles. That is what people do when promoted to manager. They take on the role they believe best displays their new position.

This role of *Hero* often motivates new managers to higher levels of activity because of the recognition they receive. It has, however, just the opposite effect on their employees. When managers monopolize decision-making and assume complete responsibility, employees often sit back and quietly smile while the boss unknowingly heads down the path of metabolic burnout. Many managers have a misguided belief that employees will be motivated by the work ethic set by the boss.

Because managers assume total responsibility for the success of their function, employees feel they have no control over the outcome of their efforts. This results in employees developing a nine-to-five attitude. In the auto industry, this is commonly stated as "do your eight and hit the gate." This passive (or sometimes aggressive) employee attitude then becomes a frequent complaint of managers, who have unwittingly caused it in the first place with their micromanagement style.

Unfortunately, I see a perpetuation of this culture in most organizations, because aspiring leaders see these managers as their role models to success. What happens is that organizations choose new managers based on their ability to conform to the corporate culture of the Hero Management Style. These new leaders further reinforce the factorial management pattern.

In order to attract the high-performing, entrepreneurial-minded, independent-thinking, team-focused employees needed today, all organizations must promote leaders who are comfortable with truly empowering their staff. To achieve this, corporations must transform their culture to one that does not reward individual heroism. They must promote and encourage managers who will supervise each staff member according to the level of competency the employee has reached. Competency level is based on the employee's ability to do the job and their eagerness to take on higher levels of responsibility and independence.

Organizations that do not recognize the new reality will end up paying higher wages, experiencing lower levels of productivity, and ultimately end up losing their best and most promising talent.

People today want to work for leaders who inspire them, not bosses who control them!

## Dynamic Coaching©

Coaching is a process, not an annual event. It is a process that unlocks the potential of an individual and maximizes his or her performance. Dynamic Coaching© is based on the belief that effectiveness results from behaving in ways that are appropriate to the demands of the situation and the competency of the employee.

The process involves the coach determining the employees' level of competence, where they want to be, and what they need to do to get there. It also consists of different phases, with each phase influencing the type of coaching intervention needed.

The coaching process developed is both simple and effective. Successful implementation, however, is dependent on your ability to assess the level of motivation and competence of the employee. In addition, you must take extreme care at each phase regarding the type of coaching behavior you apply. Accepting the premise that our objective is to have employees who are highly competent, motivated, and enthusiastic, let us illustrate a model to help you achieve this result.

*The true measure of a manager can be determined by how they treat their subordinates.*

My friend and fellow trainer Karen Lee approaches the coaching concept this way: "A person is a process not a product." People have the capacity to learn new concepts and build new skills from birth to death. In our world of work, and even in life in general, anything that another person says or does to us has an impact on our:

- **Self-Esteem**: The love we have for ourselves, with or without "warts."

- **Self-Confidence**: Our internal belief in our abilities.

- **Sense of Identity**: Who we believe we really are.

A manager or supervisor has tremendous power to affect any or all of an employee's pieces of self. A manager who disciplines a person in front of others, a trainer who shows impatience when a person is a little slow to learn, or a parent who tells their children they are stupid, affects all of the pieces.

Leaders by definition are people who influence the behaviors of others. They have a profound responsibility to influence positively. They should enhance and maintain the self-esteem, self-confidence, and sense of identity of the people for whom they are responsible. They must not detract from any of the fundamental human pieces of self. Let's put Karen's thoughts and my concepts to a practical but simple application.

## Coaching for Bicycle-Riding Competence

To describe the model, there are numerous stories I could use, but I will use an analogy that is easiest for most people to relate to. Think back to a time when you have taught a child to ride a bicycle. It may have been a son, daughter, little brother, little sister, or even a neighborhood child.

If you go back to that point in time, you will remember that the first phase of this process was when, perhaps, the child came to you and said, "Buy me a bike; I need a bike." You may have pointed that the child couldn't ride a bike. The response may have been, "Yes I can! Yes I can!" We all know that children sometimes stretch the truth regarding their abilities. If you took the child at their word, you might have purchased an expensive bike and given it to them saying, "Here, go ride it." If in fact you did that, the child probably responded, "I really can't. I need you to teach me," showing a reluctance or unwillingness to actually ride the bike.

Like the child, some employees stretch the truth on their resumes. Instead of assessing actual competency, however, many managers believe the resume and give the new employee an important responsibility at which they ultimately fail. The manager is left wondering what happened.

Although the child may have been eager to become a great and independent bicycle rider and had the *capability* to become one, at that moment they were reluctant to take on the responsibility. At that stage, the reluctance is because of lack of skill and confidence.

Later on, I am going to relate this analogy to what happens in the process of working with employees and taking them through the development stages.

Remember, the objective you have as a bicycle-riding coach is to have a child who is a knowledgeable, skilled, safe, enthusiastic, flexible, self-motivated and independent bicycle rider about whom you do not have to worry. In order to do this, you must understand the process of effective coaching.

Over the past 50 years, many management consultants and behavioral psychologists have been developing theories and mapping the different styles that managers use. Each of the theories built on the previous and took it to a new level. Great work has been done by: McGregor, Fielder, Maslow, Korman, Blake and Mouton, Hershey, Blanchard, Hertzberg, and Lafferty.

Most of these management gurus divided managers' behavior into two categories. One category is whether leaders engage in task-oriented behaviors, which results in high directive or low directive behavior. The second category is whether leaders focus on socio-emotional behavior that results in high or low interpersonal behavior. In that model, there are the following four leadership styles.

1. High directive and low interpersonal.

2. High directive and high interpersonal.

3. Low directive and high interpersonal.

4. Low directive and low interpersonal.

Correspondingly, employees' competency is determined by two dimensions:

1. Can they do the job? *(their ability)*

2. Do they want do the job? *(their eagerness)*

This results in four levels of competency:

1. Unable and reluctant.

2. Unable and eager.

3. Able and reluctant.

4. Able and eager.

A person's ability is determined by their education, experience, training, track record, knowledge, innovative thinking, ability to plan, creativity, task skills, and decision-making judgment. The psychological attributes that will determine an employee's eagerness are: self-confidence, motivation level, commitment, assertiveness, co-operation, activity level, and flexibility. Think back to the "Pillars of Competency" discussed on page 139.

As a bicycle riding coach, the objective is to have a child who is a highly competent bicycle rider – one or both able and eager to ride on their own. In order to achieve this, an adult instinctively knows exactly the behaviors in which to engage. We use these great leadership abilities in many daily aspects of our lives, such as raising our children, coaching a minor league team, coordinating scouts, or even in volunteer roles. In an organizational or corporate setting, however, when we are promoted to management, we do not always consider what we inherently know is great leadership, and engage in behavior that we subconsciously feel is the right thing to do.

Back to that aspiring bicycle rider. At this point, you have determined the child is unable and fairly reluctant to get on that bike and independently ride it down the street. We call this phase *Competency "1"*. Do not mistake this reluctance as an unwillingness to actually become a great bicycle rider; it is just a lack of confidence experienced at this point in time.

So what coaching style should you use? When asked, the response is often high interpersonal and low directive. But if you actually gave the child lots of socio-emotional, supportive behavior—encouragement not to worry, praise for taking this important step and making such progress, reassurance for how well they were going to do — the child would still not be able (or confident) to get on the bicycle and ride it. What they needs at this time is lots of "high-directive" behavior — just to be told what to do. This gives the child a sense of security.

What you probably did was, in a fairly stern and directive voice, instructed the child to sit on the seat, put his or her left foot on one pedal, right foot on the other pedal, both hands on the handle bars, and to follow specific instructions as you started to push the bike down the street. As you pushed, you continued to give the child lots of direction, but very few assurances in the form of not letting him or her fall or get hurt. This is the high directive, low interpersonal coaching style I refer to as **Instructing**. Just tell them what to do.

As you continued to push the child down the street, giving instructions on what to do next, you observed that the child was actually following your instructions and achieving small accomplishments. As the child achieved small degrees of proficiency, you probably encouraged them, starting mildly and increasing the recognition and reinforcement as the child became even more proficient with some of the tasks.

After you had run up and down the street a couple of dozen times, pushing the bike while continuing to instruct and increasing the level of feedback, perhaps you became tired and said, "Let's take a rest." At this point, the child probably said, "No, let's keep going; I want to keep going." This certainly shows high enthusiasm and confidence, but remember, it cannot yet be translated into ability. I refer to this stage as *Competency "2"*.

The coaching style you probably engaged in at this stage was both "high interpersonal" and "high directive." This is the style that requires the most sensitivity and effort on your part. It is also the most energy draining. The "high interpersonal" behavior came in the form of encouragement and compliments on how well the child was doing. The "high directive" behavior came in the form of explaining the importance of taking the time to rest, the consequences of not taking one step at a time, and the importance of understanding the big picture. I call this coaching style **Guiding**. Show them.

After an appropriate rest, the child climbed back on the bicycle, you reviewed some of the things learned, and you explained additional skills until the child got to the point where you knew that the child was now able. It was your responsibility to decide when the child was actually able. The same holds true in organizations; it is the manager's responsibility to determine when the employee is able to take on a task.

At this point, you said, "I am going to let go now. "The child responded loudly, "NO! Don't let go!" When people develop from the unable but eager stage, to the able stage, they regress back to reluctant. They display an insecurity and lack of confidence. I call this stage *Competency "3."*

At this stage, you did not use any more directive behavior, but engaged in extremely high interpersonal behavior, gave a lot of support, and encouraged and built the child's confidence. You did this by reassuring the child, saying things like, "I let go three times already, and you didn't even notice." You also made the child comfortable by saying supportive things like, "I'll run beside you for a little while. "I call this third coaching style **Inspiring** because that *is* what you are doing – inspiring the person to develop confidence and take the next big step in his or her development, which requires assuming some risk. This is when we "let them try".

As the child wobbled away, you applauded, shouted encouragement, perhaps gathered an appreciative audience or grabbed your video camera. This inspired the child to try even harder.

Then after the child had been riding the bicycle for a few months, you probably observed that they became quite able and very eager, or *Competency "4."* Your style at that point was to "leave them alone". I call this fourth coaching style **Empowering**. This is not only low in directive behavior, but also low in interpersonal behavior, other than a little encouragement when positive behavior is observed

(such as attention to safety, care for the bicycle and proactive problem solving.)

### This is the secret to being a
### true and dynamic coach.

Every employee goes through this same set of attitudes and behaviors in their journey to becoming fully competent and they must be coached appropriately at each of these stages.

Using the appropriate coaching styles will result in not only highly competent employees, but employees who enjoy their job, enjoy coming to work, are loyal to the organization, and trust management.

When I first researched coaching models, I wanted to study professions where good coaching is imperative. There are many. One is flying. When you are boarding an aircraft, you really hope that the pilot has experienced great coaching. So, I actually went through the process of flight training.

What I discovered is that the flight instructor goes through these exact four stages of coaching, starting with "instructing" in the classroom, perhaps combined with a simulator. The instructor takes the student in the air, "guiding" him or her and providing explanation and encouragement. Then one day the student shows up and the flight instructor says, "You are now able; there is the plane, and there is the sky. Good luck!" So a very eager student gets butterflies in their stomach and becomes reluctant. At this time, the flight instructor "inspires" the student by reminding them of past successes and encourages the student by maintaining radio contact. The instructor does not do any more directing! After a number of solos, the student becomes empowered and just attends an annual medical, DoT, and instrumentation updates.

Is that the way most of us have been coached at work by our bosses? Probably not. Most of us were told very specifically what to do, how to do it, and when. Perhaps the instructions were repeated multiple times. Then we were left alone to complete our responsibilities on our own. If we made a mistake or did not do exactly as the manager expected, we were instructed again (only this time perhaps they talked more slowly) and left alone once again. If it happened a few times, we were put on a "performance appraisal", because managers believe performance appraisals will fix everything.

If parents used this same coaching process to teach a child to ride a bike—told them what to do ("Put your hands here, feet here, keep your balance, and pedal hard"), then let the child go, the result would most likely be the child crashing to the ground. Then, using a process similar to that between manager and employees, the parent would instruct the child again, this time talking more slowly. Again, it would end in disaster. The third time, the parent would shout at the child, or put them on a performance appraisal, because we know performance appraisals will fix everything.

If, in fact, you coached a child this way, you would end up with a child who was a mediocre bicycle rider, or had no motivation to even go near a bicycle. More importantly, the child would not have any trust in you and what you were trying to teach them. If someone asked this child what was going on, they might reply that you were *out to get* me or maybe even *trying to kill* me!

Well, the same thing happens at work, when we coach our employees using only two styles – instructing and empowering. We end up with people who are not motivated to take responsibility and who feel their management is out to get them.

The proper coaching alignment is depicted as follows:

| EMPLOYEE COMPETENCE | COACHING STYLE |
| --- | --- |
| Unable & Reluctant | Instructing |
| Unable & Eager | Guiding |
| Able & Reluctant | Inspiring |
| Able & Eager | Empowering |

As employees develop through each of these competency levels, their level of motivation also evolves through the hierarchy described earlier. My Dynamic Coaching Model© appears as follows:

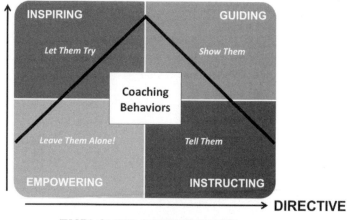

Just because an employee had similar employment experience elsewhere does not mean that in this role they will naturally be top quality, self-motivated, enthusiastic, competent employees; the availability of those individuals is usually scarce and unpredictable. iLeaders make ordinary people perform better than they seem capable of, to bring out whatever strengths they have, and to use each employee's own internal strength to inspire them to greatness.

*"All management skills are learnable;*
*you can learn any skill you need to achieve*
*any business goal you can set for yourself.*
*There are no limits!"*

- Brian Tracy

## Answers to the Management Situations

Earlier in the chapter (pp. 137-138), you answered several questions. The following are the solutions to those questions.

| Question | Correct Answer | Reasoning |
|---|---|---|
| **1** | (c)   Let the team develop and implement their own recommendations<br><br>**Employee Competency**: C4<br>**Coaching Style**: Empower | These people have experience and have made changes before. They are eager, work well together, know what has to be done, and consistently do what is required. Leave them alone! |
| **2** | (c)   Review his role and responsibilities then supervisor closely<br><br>**Employee Competency**: C1<br>**Coaching Style**: Instruct | This employee does not seem to be able to achieve objectives, and is not showing any eagerness towards improving. Just tell him what has to be done, how it has to be done and by when. |
| **3** | (d)   Encourage the team's involvement in decision-making but ensure objectives are met by explaining performance requirements<br><br>**Employee Competency**: C2<br>**Coaching Style**: Guide | The team is at a competency 2 and should be guided. This will ensure continued productivity but at the same time begin to connect (humanize) the environment. |
| **4** | (b)   Encourage her to develop the change process and ask her how she might organize the implementation<br><br>**Employee Competency**: C3<br>**Coaching Style**: Inspire | This employee seems to know what she is doing (able), but just needs some encouragement (inspiration) to help build her confidence. |

I hope you are now getting an idea about how you as a manager must adapt your coaching style to the needs of the employees. The role of a manager is to develop competent employees. But that causes us to ask: What competencies are important for managers themselves to have?

An organization with whom I work, Human Synergistics®, has determined through extensive research that there are 14 competencies that all managers need in order to succeed. Human Synergistics® compiled these via a survey asking CEOs of North America's leading corporations what competencies they felt were most important for success in the future. The three main categories are:

1. **Task Skills**
2. **Interpersonal Skills**
3. **Personal Skills**

These skills are broken down into 14 key competency areas as follows:

### 1. Task Skills

*There are six task skills as follows:*

### 1.1 Problem Solving *Recognizing and Solving Problems*

This ability involves recognizing and analyzing problems, dealing with competing issues, approaching unforeseen circumstances, selecting unpopular or risky courses of action, reacting to complicated problems and situations, and working with others to solve complex problems.

### 1.2 Time Management *Allocating & Using Time Effectively*

Time management involves allocating time to the right things, dealing with the relationship between when things should be done and when they are done, making estimates regarding the amount of time needed to complete a task, "clearing up" identified problems in a timely manner, making sure that important issues are covered in meetings and discussions, staying focused on critical activities, and pacing one's work day.

### 1.3 Planning *Providing Direction & Scheduling Activities*

This skill involves developing detailed plans, delineating and documenting the steps needed to implement a decision, anticipating events and specifying appropriate courses of action, making plans regarding tasks people are to accomplish on a daily basis, defining priorities or major steps to be taken when introducing a change or new project, and developing and communicating strategies to deal with unforeseen consequences.

### 1.4 Goal Setting *Establishing Goals & Objectives*

Goal Setting involves setting objectives for the work group or unit; focusing objectives on things employees can control; establishing specific, concrete, and clear objectives; setting objectives well ahead of decisions about who is going to do what; developing measurable and quantifiable objectives; clearly specifying priorities; and using goals and objectives to actively monitor performance.

### 1.5 Performance Leadership *Motivating Performance & Personal Development*

This skill involves structuring employees' work to make it motivating and interesting; evaluating performance by providing a sense of accomplishment and direction; assigning challenging work; motivating employees to maximize the quality and quantity of their work; setting challenging, reasonable, and fair performance standards; recognizing and rewarding good performance; and tailoring rewards to personal needs and interests.

### 1.6 Organizing *Assigning Responsibilities & Coordinating Tasks*

Organizing involves minimizing duplication of effort, assigning authority to others that is clear and appropriate to their job responsibilities, giving people the authority necessary to meet their responsibilities, organizing tasks to ensure that those responsible have the necessary resources, assigning tasks to those who are most qualified, assigning people the tasks that complement their existing activities, and ensuring that the tasks performed by the staff "fit together."

### 2. Interpersonal Skills

*There are five interpersonal skills as follows:*

### 2.1 Team Development *Promoting Teamwork & Cooperation*

Skilled team development involves creating a cooperative work climate, helping people work together toward shared objectives, developing individual work goals in relation to group goals, encouraging group members to pitch in and help one another, promoting group discussion and collaboration, focusing on the progress of the group and members' contributions when monitoring individual performance, and designing and organizing special assignments and new projects around teams.

## 2.2 Delegation *Decentralizing in Order to Empower Others*

This skill involves assuming a general approach to tasks and allowing work group members to draw up the specifics; giving people freedom in determining how to get the job done; allowing group members to decide who does what; emphasizing general guidelines when assigning tasks, then enabling people to proceed using their own judgment; giving employees the autonomy and flexibility to respond to problems; and using plans and strategies in a flexible way to allow people to make changes and respond to unanticipated events.

## 2.3 Participation *Sharing Power & Involving Others*

Participation involves evaluating suggestions on the basis of merit, not source; being open to ideas from others; helping people feel free to share their opinions and perspectives; making decisions affecting the work group only after sharing and seeking information from people in the group; sincerely asking how things are going, acknowledging difficulties, and factoring them into one's decisions; making decisions involving different ways of doing things in consultation with those responsible for making the change; and addressing complex problems by encouraging the participation of those with the necessary information and expertise.

## 2.4 Integrating Differences *Accepting & Resolving Conflict*

This skill involves settling work group arguments by deciding what is correct based on facts, instead of on who holds what position; treating disagreements as healthy expressions of different viewpoints; allowing disagreements to be expressed as a means of generating ideas and improving things; disagreeing with others only by paying attention to their ideas and openly sharing one's own; handling differences of opinion by questioning others to explore reasons for the differences; working on conflicts by paying equal concern to the needs of others and one's own needs; and mediating disagreements by reducing the sources of conflict (e.g. misunderstandings or communication breakdowns).

## 2.5 Providing Feedback *Facilitating & Encouraging Growth*

Providing proper feedback involves being helpful and supportive when talking to others about their work, discussing performance by complimenting the good and helping to improve weaker areas, helping others to grow and develop by providing constructive feedback regularly, providing support and understanding when people make mistakes, focusing on strengths that can be developed in specific ways, and offering feedback and advice that emphasizes things the recipient can do something about.

## 3. Personal Skills

*There are three personal skills as follows:*

### 3.1 Stress Processing *Managing Crises & Reducing Stress*

This skill involves seeking out and discussing suggestions calmly and openly when under stress or dealing with a crisis; solving a complicated problem by staying in control, using the information available, and making a rational decision; reacting to things "going wrong" by calmly trying to correct the situation; coping with the unexpected by remaining in good humor and working on the problem until it's resolved; addressing a build-up of little problems by staying objective and working to resolve each issue; putting aside stressful situations and moving on to the next activity; and interacting with others and approaching one's work in a way that minimizes stress for oneself and others.

### 3.2 Maintaining Integrity *Gaining Trust & Confidence*

Maintaining integrity involves keeping your word and commitments, speaking the truth while being believable, respecting confidences, "telling it like it is," supporting and implementing decisions agreed upon in conversation or formal meetings, using your influence appropriately to represent the concerns of employees and promote their interests, and sharing the credit with group members when the work group carries out an assignment particularly well.

### 3.3 Commitment *Demonstrating Loyalty & Responsibility*

This skill involves accepting heavy workloads without complaint; expressing trust and confidence in the organization and top management; applying oneself and giving a great amount to the job; doing anything to help in an emergency or when problems arise; setting an excellent example of dedication to the job; emphasizing the larger organization when setting objectives, establishing priorities, and interpreting organizational strategies for the work group; and supporting proposals that would benefit the organization, regardless of their effect on one's own career objectives.

## Human Synergistics®

Human Synergistics® has determined that four of these competencies are essential for a manager to provide effective coaching. These are as follows:

- Providing Feedback
- Performance Leadership
- Delegation
- Goal Setting

These are essential because they capture the essence of a manager's attitude and skills towards enabling the growth and development of others.

Human Synergistics® has a 360° survey process known as MEPS™ (Management Effectiveness Profile System), which can be used to assess the level of proficiency a manager has achieved in each of these competencies. This system also provides a step-by-step method of personal development, which can be used by managers to increase their proficiency in these critical areas.[*]

---

[*]*MEPS™ (Management Effectiveness Profile System). All rights reserved. For further information or if you would like to complete one of the MEPS™, please contact info@ethos.ca*

## But I Don't Have Time

So often, I hear leaders say, "Look, our managers have to hit the road running. We don't have time to send them to training programs." Social scientists say that only one out of every 100 people (1%) say they have enough time to accomplish everything they need to accomplish in the day. Forty percent of all people admit they need about 25% more time to finish everything they need to do every day. 50% want more time.

We have been conditioned with certain beliefs about time management, and these have existed for centuries. *The first belief revolves around activity.* Contrary to our conditioned belief, activity does not mean achievement. The two concepts should not be confused. I know you must have activity to have achievement, but not all activity is productive activity. You need motion to achieve movement, but not all motion is movement. We have all heard the old expressions that active people get the most done. "When in doubt, go faster." Wrong! The people who get things done are the ones who set goals and prioritize.

*The next belief about time is that the higher the decision-level, the better decision that is made.* Actually, the closer you are to the situation, the better the decision. Sometimes that happens from the bottom up and not the top down.

*The third belief is that people who are paid more make better decisions.* Wrong again. They are paid more because they produce more. You deserve your pay, no matter how good or bad your job is. You deserve your life no matter how good or bad it is.

*The fourth belief is the longer you take to decide, the better the decision.* Not always. Sometimes I find the ready-fire-aim philosophy is the best strategy. Microsoft is notorious for doing this. Dale Carnegie said if you are right 51% of the time you are a winner. Make a decision and then adjust.

So many people, especially the analytical types, suffer from "paralysis by analysis". They defend their situation by saying they need more facts. More often than not, they lack courage to decide. That is why iLeaders are good decision makers and make more money. They are more afraid of not deciding than they are of failing. In his book *Blink*, Malcolm Gladwell makes the case that spontaneous decisions are often as good as – or even better than – carefully planned and considered ones.

*The fifth belief is about delegation.* Some managers say, "I don't have time to delegate. I can do it more quickly myself." Not only are they heading for burn-out, but they are also depriving their employees of much-needed development and job satisfaction.

*Belief six is that the most efficient person is the most effective.* It is an old debate: efficiency versus effectiveness. The answer lies in a correct blend of both. A poor long-term strategy for an organization is to spend time trying to do something more cheaply (or more effectively) when it should not be done at all. Effectiveness is about doing the *right* things efficiently.

*Finally, the belief I encounter the most: No one can do it better than me.* Many executives suffer from this problem. They think that tasks are achieved faster and better if they do them themselves. This is particularly true for entrepreneurs who started with nothing and built a multi-million dollar organization. Perhaps you are terrific at stacking boxes in the back of a truck, or closing a sale with a customer on the phone, but when you do that, you should pay yourself that wage and not the wage of an executive. iLeaders are successful *because* of their actions and not *in spite* of those actions.

## Bosses Without a Heart

In their book *The Corporate Coach*, James B. Miller and Paul Brown asked for entries to a "Worst Boss" contest. He received over 1000 entries from employees who thought their bosses were heartless. Among many of the stories he received were actions like:

- Hiding or altering an employee's time card.
- Searching employees' lockers and personal belongings.
- Verbally abusing employees until they started to cry.

One of the worst was an entry from a worker who said their boss had refused to call 911 before 5:00 p.m. to look after an employee who had died at his desk; the manager reasoned that it would disrupt the office and be unproductive.

A number of years ago in Montreal, a woman was attacked in the parking lot of a company. She was left lying unconscious within eyesight of the company's employees. When they asked if they could go and assist her, their boss told them not to get involved and that they were not allowed to leave their workstations during company time. The employees assisted the woman anyway, and she was taken to the hospital.

In my own surveys, I have found that a good manager can actually be the greatest long-term motivator of employees. An Industry Week survey found that "a manager with Vision and Values" was a top motivator.

Another Swedish study done in 2008 found people who consider their bosses to be unfair, arbitrary, inconsiderate, and generally deficient in managerial skills are at greater risk for having a cardiac event such as a heart attack.

Stress caused by bad managers adds up, increasing risk of heart problems over time, the researchers report in the Nov. 24, 2008 issue of *Occupational and Environmental Medicine*. The more competent workers ranked their managers, the lower their risk of serious heart problems.

## What is Your Coaching IQ?

*The following exercise will help you to rate your coaching behavior, and determine how much effort you are putting into developing your employees. Read each question and give yourself a score of one to five. When you are finished, add up your score and see how you compare with the results listed on the next page.*

| Never | | Sometimes | | Always |
|:---:|:---:|:---:|:---:|:---:|
| **1** | **2** | **3** | **4** | **5** |

1. Do you clarify your role and your expectations? _____

2. When you begin the coaching session, do you put the employee at ease? _____

3. Do you take the time to build trust? _____

4. Do you stay attentive and focused during the coaching session? _____

5. Do you provide appropriate support and training when needed? _____

6. Do employees report they feel you hear and understand them? _____

7. Do you ask open-ended questions to encourage an employee's opinion or suggestions? _____

8. Do you refrain from pigeonholing employees? _____

9. Do you respond authentically to employees without using techniques or canned answers? _____

10. Do you explore new possibilities or refrain from offering your solution to a problem? _____

11. Are you a good role model? _____

12. Do you provide feedback in a timely manner? _____

**Total Points** _____

### Results of Coaching IQ

**40 or above:** Congratulations. You are a competent coach who shows a genuine interest in the development of your employees. Continue to practice these coaching behaviors and you will further contribute to a constructive workplace.

**Below 40:** Review which coaching skills you do well. Determine which coaching skills you could learn and decide which of these you would be willing to practice and improve. Every time you increase your coaching skills you are contributing to a constructive workplace. Listen to others, and you will be listened to.

**Add your own:** There may be other coaching skills that you practice that are not described in the exercise. Add any skills that you believe would improve your coaching relationship.

**My coaching skills examples:**

_____

_____

**Role Model:** *Was there a coach who you encountered in the past who you felt exemplified good coaching? What were the behaviors he or she exhibited?*

_____

_____

*I believe the major difference between a successful person and everyone else is not a lack of strength, a lack of knowledge, or even a lack of will, but the absence of a great coach or mentor.*

Successful people learn from other successful people. This way of learning is known as *mentoring*. It has been around for a very long time. The concept was first recorded in Homer's epic tale, *The Odyssey*. In it, Homer describes how Odysseus entrusts his loyal advisor, a man named Mentor, with the care and education of Odysseus's infant son Telemachus.

*When you make it your mission to help others, the person you help the most is yourself.*

To find a mentor is to find a trusted advisor who can help you to determine how things work and why they are the way they are. A good mentor can also show you what is important or unimportant, and what you should or should not do.

In most organizations, mentoring is a one-on-one relationship where a senior, or experienced person becomes a wise and trusted counselor to a less experienced person. The problem with this traditional method is that one person can rarely provide the kind of support we often require. We may want diversity in what we learn, to be exposed to a variety of leadership styles, to develop lines of succession, and to increase the breadth of who we communicate with. The best way to achieve personal and business success is to build mentoring relationships with a number of people.

Recognize that mentoring should really be about creating mutual learning opportunities. You can give opportunities to, and receive opportunities from, a variety of individuals. In other words, begin networking, increase your connections, and find the right people who can help you, and discover how you can help others. Because of changes in today's workplace, not one person can provide sufficient scope to meet all our developmental needs.

*Influence cannot be achieved without the constructive use of power.*

### Power & Influence

As a leader, it is your responsibility to modify others' behaviors, in a positive way. And you want to be able to do that without working too hard. What will give you that ability is power. However, not everyone is comfortable with using each of the powers they have at their disposal. That is like a carpenter who does not use all the tools in their toolbox.

To be successful as a coach or mentor, you must be comfortable with using power. There are eight power bases that we operate from on a day-to-day basis. It is important that you are equally comfortable with using each of them.

Also remember, power is neither good or nor bad. It is how power is used that makes it good or bad. Each of the following powers is important when used appropriately, and each of these power bases is equally important.

All of the power bases fall into one of two categories. The first is *Position Power:* This is the extent to which you control distribution of rewards, punishments, and sanctions to your subordinates. This is authority that has been delegated to you by your superior.

The other is *Personal Power:* This is the extent to which you gain the confidence and respect of your people: your ability to generate cohesiveness, trust, and commitment among the people you are leading.

| Position Power | Personal Power |
|:---:|:---:|
| coercive | precedent |
| association | information |
| legitimate | expert |
| reward | connection |

### Coercive Power

The first in the ladder of position powers is *coercive power.* This is based on fear. A leader who uses coercive power induces compliance because failure to comply will lead to punishments such as undesirable work assignments, reprimands, dismissals, or loss of benefits. More subtle intimidation elements are also used, speaking loudly, aggressive body language, or singling others out in public.

On the positive side, this power is very effective when dealing with a low competency employee. For instance, we are very comfortable using this power to change the behavior of a child who is doing something dangerous like running into a busy street. We say, "Don't you ever do that again or else..." It would be ineffective to use information or exert another power in this situation. In the work environment, we have to be just as direct and say things like, "If you do not get your time sheets in by 3:00 p.m. on Friday, you will not be paid next week." Remember, this power should not be used as a threat or intimidation, but more as a natural consequence for inappropriate behavior.

### Association Power

Association Power is based on the leader's personal association with other influential or important persons inside or outside the organization. A leader who uses association power induces compliance because others aim at gaining the favor or avoiding the disfavor of said persons. Leaders who are seen with important individuals take on the aura of importance through their association.

To a child, we may say something like, "Wait until your mother gets home; then you'll be in big trouble." I should point out that association power is often used in a positive way, such as, "You did such a great job! When I have lunch with the CEO I am going to tell them what a great performer you are."

## Legitimate Power

Legitimate Power is primarily based on the position held by the leader. The higher the position, the higher the legitimate power is perceived to be. This works best with workers at competency level two. Employees are compliant because they feel a leader with legitimate power has the right, by virtue of position in the organization, to expect that his or her suggestions be followed. The leader must be comfortable with using the ornaments associated with their position: things like having a larger office, a preferred parking space, or wearing different clothing, such as a doctor's coat or a different colored hard hat. Police officers use legitimate power very effectively with their easily recognizable cars and uniforms.

Can you imagine how hard a police officer's job would be if they did not "legitimize" their power with a very specific uniform? In the office, it is just as important that managers differentiate themselves by the way they dress. It makes their job easier. For further information, read the section on "disrobing business casual" at the end of this section.

## Reward Power

Reward Power is based on the leader's ability to gain favor by providing tangible or intangible rewards to others: bonuses, promotions, favored work assignments, awards, or other personal recognition. Research has shown that if a leader focuses more on intangible rewards, there will be a more positive long-term behavior change.

## Precedent Power

Precedent Power is most effective with competency level three employees. It is based on the leader's experience and is used by showing examples of how the leader (or other workers) pulled through in similar situations. This provides employees comfort and decreases uncertainty by knowing that if similar procedures and processes are followed, everything will work out just fine. Examples include how case law is used in the courts and how pilot programs are conducted prior to making final decisions.

## Information Power

Is based on the leader's possession of, or access to, information that is perceived as valuable to others. This power influences others because they need this information or want to be "in on things." Information about others' abilities enables leaders to ask probing questions and give others the opportunity to display their skills.

## Expert Power

Is based on the leader's possession of a specific expertise, skill, ability, or knowledge that gains the respect of others. This is one of the most effective powers to use with the higher-level competency workers. A leader with expert power possesses the expertise to facilitate the work behavior of others and bring out their personal best. Respect enables a leader to influence others by displaying confidence.

This does not mean, however, that the leader has to be an expert at the task the worker is involved in. The leader's expertise lies in their ability to listen, decide, coach, and mentor. In fact, often when the leader is more of a technical expert, it actually de-motivates the worker and they just give up.

### Connection Power

Is based on the leader's personal traits and their ability to make a personal connection of trust with others. A leader scoring high in Connection Power is generally liked and admired by others because of their personality and communication style. This admiration and identification with the leader leads to a charismatic connection, which influences the workers positively.

Connection Power is basically communicating in the way the worker needs to be communicated with. This will foster trust between managers and employees.

There are appropriate times when each of these power bases is generally used. For instance:

| In a Climate of: | This Power: | Provides: |
| --- | --- | --- |
| Despair | **Connection** | Hope |
| Conflict | **Expert** | Certainty |
| Ignorance | **Information** | Enlightenment |
| Indecision | **Precedence** | Comfort |
| Uncertainty | **Reward** | Reinforcement |
| Disorder | **Legitimate** | Stability |
| Anxiety | **Association** | Security |
| Crisis | **Coercive** | Direction |

*"The sole advantage of power is
that you can do more good"*

- Baltasar Gracian

An example of how Legitimate Power has been neutralized in the workplace today is the fad towards dressing down. Following is a bit of history on why that has happened and the effect it has had.

## Disrobing Business Casual

*Many leaders are starting to wonder how far the "dress casual" revolution will go.* To discover this answer, we must understand what started it, and more importantly, what effect it is having on our ability to get things done.

As leaders and managers, our success depends on other people doing things for us. To be successful at this depends on our ability to modify employees' behavior. We want to be able to do this by expending the least amount of effort on our part. Think of a police officer who wants you to pull over. When they are standing on the street in full uniform (wearing a cap), we do not think twice; we just pull over.

However, if that same officer, with the same authority, was wearing casual clothes, most of us would not even think of pulling over. Some might even speed up to get past more quickly. If police officers did not wear uniforms, their jobs would become very difficult indeed.

The same applies in business. As managers, we must motivate employees to do their duties. Studies have shown that if managers are not wearing appropriate "uniforms," employees will not always do what managers ask. In fact, some managers have reported that employees may do just the opposite. Managers tell me if they are required to discipline an employee, they will definitely wear a suit that day. It helps the process go more smoothly.

So why did we begin dressing casually? Wearing casual clothes started in the high-tech industry. During the 1980s, most of the growing entrepreneurial high-tech firms shipped their products out on Fridays. So when things became really busy, everyone in the company rolled up their sleeves to help out. It was more practical to do this while wearing jeans and sporty clothes. Fridays then became "Casual Fridays" by tradition.

After that, many other organizations caught on to the fad, and it seemed to extend to almost every day. Little by little, the attire became so relaxed that some companies found they had to implement guidelines prohibiting halter tops, shorts, T-shirts, and so on. By this time, however, the casual revolution was entrenched. Since the dot.com firms normally hired young people who did not have past experience with traditional business attire, they just embedded casual dress as a way of life. I have heard that in some corporations, employees will wear a suit once a week on a regular basis, just so their management does not know when they might have a job interview scheduled with a competitor.

Now other problems are emerging. Just like the police officer who would have trouble stopping a car without a uniform, without business attire, managers do not command the same respect and behavior from subordinates. Nurses are not getting the same respect from doctors or patients, store clerks are held in lesser regard and sometimes abused by customers, teachers find themselves harassed by students, and leaders find they have to work twice as hard as they did in the past to motivate people.

Because of this, a backlash against business-casual attire has begun. As an example, a group of retailers plan to launch "dress-up Thursdays," hoping to get employees to wear suits at least one day a week. There are those who think "sloppy casual" attire in the office is linked to absenteeism, low productivity, flirtation, and lack of decorum. Casualness has reached the point of bare navels and tight sweaters. For women to dress professionally, the guideline is to be professionally feminine.

Dr. Allen Konopacki, President of INCOMM Research & Sales Training, a Chicago-based trade show and consulting company, said the "dress-down" style in many corners of the business world just degenerated into a rumpled, unkempt look. "Customers can no longer relate to the dress-down look as being casual—they look at it as being sloppy," he said.

Konopacki noted that ties are now familiar fixtures around the necks of Microsoft Chairman Bill Gates and Oracle Founder and CEO Larry Ellison.

*Dressing down is out –*
*Dressing up is in.*

# iLeader Profile

## James Malliaros

*James Malliaros, the Senior Vice President for Sales at Universal Studios Canada is a driving force in the company's growth, particularly in the home entertainment side of the overall business.*

*He has had a variety of roles within the organization since 1993 and currently heads up all sales, category management, direct retail planning, sales planning, and communication. In addition, he also oversees the Canadian digital delivery business including electronic sell-through and EVOD.*

The pattern I keep seeing over and over again with everyone I have interviewed is that the entrepreneurial spirit, need for independence, and control over their lives begins at an early age. James worked in various roles from the age of 13, from pumping gas, delivering pizza, and working at a factory to anything at all that gave him financial independence and personal control. At the age of 21, he opened a '50s-themed diner called the Pink Cadillac Café and sold it two years later, doubling his investment. That's when he really got a taste for business and realized the importance of keeping customers happy.

James learned about leadership through many years of working in a variety of roles and owning his own business. He also learned from friends and relatives who were all very entrepreneurial. His best friend built one of the most successful construction companies in Melbourne, Australia.

This individual has been a constant sounding board for James over the years. Others who significantly influenced him include Mike Lazaridis, who co-founded RIM (Black-Berry). James found the feat both inspiring and visionary. He also observed Isadore Sharp, the founder of the Four Seasons hotel chain. James feels Isadore's obsession with the customer experience is incredible; "he was way ahead of his time." James also admired the Division Manager of Australian entertainment giant Village Roadshow, where James worked. "This leader was incredible, a pure genius in terms of movie marketing." The manager now runs Disney Australia.

James's current boss, Steve Dorman, has also been a great mentor and friend. Steve has a unique ability to nurture and understand people at every level. However, it was James's dad who influenced his overall work ethic, which gave him the competitive edge needed to succeed in this industry.

James feels that although all chapters in this the book are critical, his natural strength is in the area of coaching people. He genuinely likes all people and is fascinated with them and what it takes to help them grow and be successful. He feels to keep people motivated, there is a need to constantly focus on praise and recognition and celebrate success.

If there were one area he would have put more focus on in his early days it would have been to learn to be more patient: Patient with people who were different, patient in dealing with complex business challenges, and patient with himself and his own personal limitations.

James is absolutely not a believer in using money as a way to motivate people. One must provide a balanced approach, especially today: "It is more about flexible work arrangements, corporate values, culture, career growth, and fun," he says. "Equitable compensation is important but will become less important as we continue to find ways to make the overall work experience and environment rewarding and productive." Universal rarely loses people because of compensation issues.

James feels the new generations and the mosaic of people from all over the world are wonderful. This trend is creating the ability to share knowledge about each other and to celebrate the differences that each community brings to the organization. We are privileged to have this opportunity. In addition, the millennial cohorts that have begun to enter our work environment have also changed things; you now have several generations all working together in a collaborative manner. He feels that a company which is able to harness this diversity can really increase their competitive advantage. The secret to success in the future is creating a culture that has an inclusive "one goal, one vision" approach.

James's personal model for coaching people to higher performance includes a model centered on three core strategies:

1. **Establishing Trust and Rapport**
2. **Demonstrating Concern and Respect**
3. **Listening with Empathy**

The key to implementing this successfully is preparation, conduct and follow-up.

In terms of communication, James feels most executives and people generally do not possess the awareness or the skills to deal with the many shapes and forms of communication. While it appears to be a fairly simple action, it's amazing how one single word or a delivery of words and actions can affect people for the longest time. Power and politics unfortunately play a huge role in developing communication styles and creating conflict within organizations. When you add this to the lack of training most people have had in this area, it can become extremely toxic. In business the most damaging issues are created because of communication challenges.

In the entertainment industry, a culture of adaptability and an entrepreneurial mindset is ideal. At Universal, the culture is centered on rapid change and being constantly flexible around the customer. Since it is not a highly technical environment, it's the cultural fit that makes the difference in people's success. In fact, the few employees that have failed did so largely because their personal value system was not in alignment with the organization's culture.

The thing that has contributed to James's success the most is that he is a believer in setting goals and writing them down. Every year he makes his list and keeps it handy. He believes this is the one thing that has helped him continually grow as an individual both professionally and personally. One of his favorite quotes that he lives by is this: "A person's character is determined by what it takes to upset them." James has reached a place in his life where he does not let anything upset him. He has a unique ability to always rise above the current clamor and maintain a meta-perspective on the chaos.

*Mr. Malliaros is a graduate of RMIT University in Melbourne, Australia and holds a GDM and an MBA from Athabasca University in Canada. He lives in Toronto, Ontario with his wife and three children. Before joining NBC/Universal Canada, James Malliaros served with entertainment giant Village Roadshow Corporation in Melbourne, Australia.*

# Summary

## *Chapter Three*

## Breakthrough Thoughts

- *iLeaders are great coaches.*
- *Pillars of Competency.*
- *Manage people like they are all volunteers.*

## Developing Employee Competence

- *Focus on strengths.*
- *Positive leadership.*
- *The animal school.*

## The Constructive Coach

- *Heroes not welcome.*
- *The Dynamic Coaching Model©.*
- *The eight bases of power.*
- *Disrobing business casual.*

## Management Skills Development

- *Task, intrapersonal and interpersonal.*
- *Your coaching IQ.*

# Chapter Four

## *Communicating the Message*

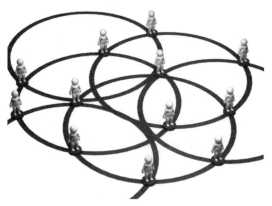

*"The majority of all problems in communications start
with misunderstandings which are created
because of conditioning and genetics."*

With our focus to become more professional in this rapidly changing, hi-tech world, we must be even more vigilant about maintaining responsive communications with all the people who are important to our success. The more the world goes hi-tech, the more we have to be proactive about becoming more hi-*touch*.

Much of today's communication is through social media networks. All generations now are engaged in Facebook, YouTube, MySpace, LinkedIn, Twitter, Plaxo, and so on. Therefore, it is even more important that we understand how significant subtleties and nuances are to the outcome of constructive communication.

Most of the activities at work depend on our ability to understand and apply effective interpersonal communication. This is true in acquiring information, giving information, offering services to clients, and collaborating with colleagues, subordinates and managers.

Communicating more efficiently is paramount to maximizing our potential. Many employers greatly value strong communicators. It could be said that they value interpersonal skills as much as technical skills. With an eye on the bottom line, they are sensitive to the fact that a great deal of money is wasted because instructions are misunderstood.

Effective interpersonal communication also plays a major role in retention management. People do not leave jobs, they leave bosses. Many people who leave say their reason is that their boss didn't understand them. They state concerns like, "My boss never listens to me," or "He tunes me out whenever I start talking," are often expressed.

*"The way we communicate with others and with ourselves ultimately determines the quality of our lives."*

- Anthony Robbins

## Macro Communication Strategies

Communication is the most important skill in life. The ability to communicate is absolutely critical for effectiveness. Aside from the fact that strong communicators have the edge in today's competitive work environment, improving our communication skills helps us to meet our basic human needs.

One of our strongest desires is to be understood. To have another person understand what we think, feel, value, love, hate, fear, believe in, and are committed to can be one of life's greatest pleasures. That is why effective interpersonal communication is such an important part of a healthy workplace.

Effective interpersonal communication is necessary to satisfy our need for recognition. The way our manager, peers, and subordinates communicate with us lets us determine how we are accepted and appreciated. It is this kind of communication that determines our *fit* within an organization. In fact, it has often been said that it is the *fit* that determines whether a person will stay or leave. Unfortunately, effective communication in the workplace is rare.

Aside from the fact that the way we communicate directly affects the bottom line and whether or not we retain our star performers, it also plays a very important role in our physical well-being. The psychological need to be understood is important for our survival. Research has shown that poor adult interpersonal relationships can contribute to hypertension and coronary disease.

We also know that our work relationships will suffer when we have trouble communicating effectively with our co-workers. In fact, the way we communicate is one of the chief causes of stress-related problems in the workplace.

It actually determines the kind of work relationships we have, and whether or not our basic needs will be met.

One of the basic needs that can be met through effective communication is our need to reduce uncertainty. We communicate to create a shared understanding of what is most important to us. As we learn more about our co-workers, and they learn more about us, we are all better able to predict each other's behavior. This helps the world become a stable place: safer, with less uncertainty.

## Effective Communication Reduces Stress

Stress is a killer. It's as simple as that. Therefore, anything you can do to reduce the negative stress in your workplace and to increase your resistance to stress will definitely increase your health and your lifespan.

People who are suffering from a stress-related problem make up almost 75% of all visits to doctors. Stress-related problems are the greatest contributor to employee absenteeism.

One study published by the Canadian Heart and Stroke Foundation revealed that 43% of Canadians suffer from stress. That means if you and a co-worker are currently reading this book, one of you is probably suffering from significant stress. The numbers are staggering. The cause is also disturbing. This study listed the main causes of stress as being related to home, family, and work.

It is easy to explain the cause of stress. Stress is defined by control. If you have control over a situation, your stress will go down. On the other hand, if you lose control, or lack control, your stress will go up.

There were studies done years ago in the airlines industry on stress. Two people are involved in safely landing a plane in a crisis situation; one is the pilot, and the other is the air traffic controller. After the crisis is over and the plane lands safely, they found that it is the air traffic controller who experiences the most stress. Even though at no time was the controller's life in danger. The studies found that the reason was because the pilot had a feeling of control, and the air traffic controller did not.

## The Human Function Curve

It seems we always talk about stress as a bad thing. In fact, if we did not have any stress in our lives, nothing would get done. As we are subjected to increased stress, our productivity goes up proportionally. Remember when did you do your best studying for final exams, or when you were most productive about preparing for a presentation for senior management.

This good, or positive stress is known as eustress, a healthy form of stress that can keep you motivated and excited about life. The opposite of eustress, and the negative kind of stress, is distress. Distress is the most commonly referred to type of stress, having negative implications.

As the accompanying graphic illustrates, if the level of stress continues to increase or lasts too long, then our productivity drops. The first signal of too much stress is feeling tired all the time, which then leads to exhaustion, then to illness. If the stress is not relieved, it could actually result in a metabolic breakdown.

# Human Function Curve

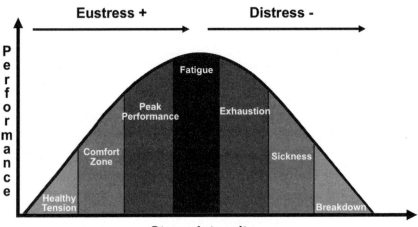

**Stress Intensity**

Many people desire consistency and predictability in the workplace. Unfortunately, in the era of downsizing, restructuring, and cutbacks, insecurity and unpredictability are part of our reality. Is it any wonder that our work environment greatly contributes to the stress in our lives simply because it is even less predictable and supportive?

The answer lies in improving the level of communication. People will feel more in control if they understand the challenges and what is expected of them.

Stress is unavoidable. Especially stress from our work environment. However, we can cope better if we have a clear understanding of goals and expectations. This can only happen if there is constant, constructive communication.

## Understand the Message

Effective communication is a two-way process. To put it simply, it is understanding and being understood. It is more than a simple process of speaking and writing clearly. It is the ability to hear and understand accurately what another person has *intended* to communicate. It is also the ability to communicate intended messages successfully and to obtain feedback to ensure the messages were received accurately.

In any relationship, people must communicate, and such communication is always subject to distortion and misunderstanding. Messages can be facts, feelings, or a combination of both. Consequently, effective communication requires an understanding and sensitivity to many aspects of the communication process such as assumptions, attitudes, and values.

Unless the parties involved have the skill and the inclination to minimize miscommunications and correct misunderstandings as they occur, a positive relationship is not likely to develop or be maintained.

*Effective communication exists between two people when the receiver interprets the sender's message in the same way the sender intended it.*

## How Important are Listening Skills?

The answer is, *very*. It is one of the most important communication skills to learn and do well. It is also the one communication skill we hear the most complaints about. Unfortunately, as stated by Beverly Kaye and Sharon Jordan-Evans in *Love 'Em or Lose 'Em: Getting Good People to Stay*, "Most managers don't really believe that listening is a critical skill. They believe that being results-oriented or customer-focused is much more important to business success than being a good listener."

Sometimes a manager may think they are a good listener when in fact they are not. They do not realize that listening is hard work. They treat listening as if it were a spectator sport. What that means is that they sit back passively and hear what the person is saying, but they are not actively involved in the listening process. Effective listening means being involved. It is active, not passive, and does not mean simply hearing. Some people protest, "I'm a good listener; I can even repeat everything he said." The problem is that these people make the incorrect assumption that the mere act of allowing the person to talk is equal to listening. They assume that simply hearing and remembering means understanding. They take listening skills for granted and often assume they are better at listening than they really are.

Many employers do recognize the importance of good listening skills. They read the studies that show employees are required to spend most of their time listening. In today's e-mail world, voicemail and face-to-face communication demand a great deal of our attention and energy. However, the fact that employees listen at only an efficiency rating of 25% means a lot of wasted money, and a negative effect on the bottom line, due to misunderstood instructions.

Even in the world of sales, where traditionally people are taught to speak more effectively and go for the close, they know that salespeople who ask the right questions and truly listen to the responses (not just the words) will eventually make more sales. The emphasis should be on letting the customer talk while the salesperson listens. The focus has become: "First find out what they want, understand their needs, and build a relationship." The same is true in the area of customer care. No wonder there has been a growing trend in the business community of sending employees to listening skills courses.

Of course we have all heard the phrase, "You have one mouth and two ears. They should be used in that proportion." That is easy to say but a lot harder to practice.

When it comes to communication skills, listening is the hardest one of all. I have been teaching interpersonal communication skills for many years, and even though I pride myself on my ability in this area, there is still much room for improvement.

Another major problem is our limited attention span. We live in a talk-oriented society. We get inundated with all kinds of communication babble that is sometimes difficult to escape. Have you ever noticed how the volume of a television commercial seems louder than the program you're watching? This is the advertiser's attempt to stop you from tuning out.

This situation is amplified by the new social media and the need to keep our messages to 140 characters or less. Now that will become the norm, and it will be even harder to "listen" longer than that.

We are also used to being entertained. How often have you found it difficult to listen to a person who spoke in a monotone, or whose voice did not sound pleasant? Maybe you found the subject matter boring so you escaped and let your mind wander to more pleasant thoughts. Perhaps you will admit that unless the speaker is interesting and can engage you with their style or topic, you just won't listen.

## Improving Listening Skills

Here are some other reasons why it is so hard to improve your listening skills, along with some suggestions:

1. **I'm not interested.** Do you ever find yourself thinking, "This stuff he's talking about is really boring," or "I hope she's finished talking soon so I can get back to what I was doing." If so, you might as well accept that you are not listening. To improve your skill, simply search for something of interest to you. Develop a frame of mind that is curious and know that no matter what the other person is talking about, there is always something worth understanding.

2. **I get tired when I'm listening.** We all do. As a matter of fact, listening takes energy: even more energy than talking. So do yourself a favor and exercise your mind. Develop your capacity to listen. When you work at getting yourself in physical shape, you gradually increase the level of difficulty of your exercises, and eventually what used to be hard for you, becomes easier. Improving your capacity to listen works in the same way. Every time you raise the bar, and stick with it, you will improve. You will have more energy to listen.

3. **I get distracted.** Do you find yourself being easily distracted by the sounds around you, like other people's conversation, the phone ringing, or noisy machinery? If that's the case, close your door, or find a quiet place so you can focus on the other person.

**4. I can't get a word in.** How often do you jump in and offer your opinion, or start to talk about your agenda? If the answer is even, "just sometimes," then you're not listening. You cannot listen if you are talking. You are also not listening while you are preparing your response. So, this one is easy — stop talking!

**5. I find myself thinking about other things.** This one is a major problem. Did you know that we are not really designed to be good listeners? Most people talk at a speed of about 125 words per minute, yet we think at a much faster rate. Research shows that we can think at a rate four times faster than a person can speak. That means your mind can think of about four words while the other person has only been able to say one. The answer is, of course, concentration. Focus on what is being said. Pay attention to the whole message, including the non-verbal communication.

Difficult as it is, listening skills can be improved. Better listening among co-workers will lead to greater understanding and a more constructive workplace.

## Non-Verbal Communication

What you *do* can have more impact on your communication then what you *say*. According to Dr. Albert Mehrabian, a U.C.L.A. researcher in the field of verbal and nonverbal messages, your communication effectiveness depends on three critical factors:

**VERBAL:** The message itself, the words you say.

**VOCAL:** The tone, variety, projection, and resonance of your voice.

**VISUAL:** What people see, specifically in your body language.

His research also revealed that visual factors, especially during the initial stages of a meeting, were the most influential. Body language has more of an impact than the tone, variety and projection of your voice and the actual words you use. You can believe that old saying, "A picture is worth a thousand words." It has been proven by research. Workshop participants often ask me if that means that what they say is not important. My tongue-in-cheek reply is usually, "Politicians have known about this for years. Forget content—as long as they look good and sound inspiring, people will vote for them."

## I Do and I Understand

To prove the importance of nonverbal and visual impressions, try a little experiment with a friend: Sit facing the other person, look him or her in the eye, and say, "I agree." As you say the words, however, frown and shake your head from side to side as if you are signaling "no." If that doesn't confuse them, I don't know what will.

It seems that we place greater belief in what we see than what we hear. If you have had the experience of talking to a person who is not familiar with your language, you know that a lot can be interpreted from nonverbal messages. We often make assumptions about a person's friendliness and how approachable they are by the way they look.

So remember, even though you're not saying anything, you're still communicating. It is true when they say it's impossible *not* to communicate.

The most effective way to get your message across as clearly as possible, is to combine the content of your message with a correspondingly appropriate nonverbal message. This kind of communication is called *congruent sending*. When the content and the feeling you show are both the same, there is less of a chance of being misunderstood.

Do not try to hide your feelings, since a lack of visual cues will make interpretation more difficult. These signals represent a major resource in your ability to be understood. Combine these signals with the corresponding and appropriate words and you increase the power and effectiveness of your communications.

### Some Helpful Hints

We're all familiar with the saying, "You never have a second chance to make a good first impression." Valuable and often lasting impressions are made within the first few minutes, even seconds, of contact with people. Your best efforts at communication may be wasted if you do not concentrate on creating a positive communication climate. Your tone of voice, your expression, and your apparent receptiveness to the responses of others all have tremendous impact on the success or failure of the communication process.

Some helpful hints to practice in order to create a positive first impression are:

1. Tune the world out and tune people in.

2. Put people at ease and make them feel important.

3. Get people talking about themselves.

4. Be sensitive and ask non-threatening questions.

5. Hold eye contact and listen to how people feel.

The important message here is to quickly set up a communication process where they talk and you listen. People will be more responsive to you if you take their interests and needs into account.

### How People Make Meaning

By now you realize how difficult it can be to understand and be understood. I have described how active listening, nonverbal communication, and congruent sending will greatly improve your chances of making this happen. There is another factor that you should consider. It is popularly known by the name Neuro-Linguistic Programming (NLP). NLP was made famous by Richard Bandler and John Grinder.

Two of the original books written on the subject were Richard Bandler and John Grinder's book *Frogs into Princes* and *Practical Magic* by Steve Lankton. Basically, the authors maintain that human beings transmit and receive messages through three primary representational systems. They are: Visual (see), Auditory (hear), and Kinesthetic (touch). We use these three systems to process information and understand our world, yet we have what is called a "lead" system through which we represent our experiences. This results in us having differences in what is called "digital presentation." The following is an example of how these presentations will differ according to a person's learning style.

- **Visual:** "This looks really good and clear to me." "I see what you are saying."

- **Auditory:** "Tell me in more detail." "This sounds really good to me."

- **Kinesthetic:** "This feels really good to me." "I feel really good about what we are doing."

Optimum communication takes place when all three systems are engaged in the process.

## The Birds©

Over the years, I have observed many things about the differences in the way people communicate. I have attended numerous seminars, read many books, conducted informal studies, and even became certified to teach models on behavioral science. These were all designed to improve our understanding of each other's personalities, attitudes and behaviors.

Many seminars miss the most important point: How can we quickly identify and adapt our communication for a wide range of diverse individuals to be more effective in achieving mutual goals?

I have spent the last 20 years developing a model that I have successfully used to help people create powerful communication connections. It is presented here in the hope that by reading this you will develop skills on how to quickly identify, through a variety of signals, what another person requires from you when they are sending messages. You will also understand how to modify your style to one which best suits the individuals you are trying to motivate, or change the behaviors you are attempting to influence.

To make this document simple, easier to follow, and more efficient to relate, each of the communication styles is assigned the name of a bird. The attributes of the bird I have assigned to each of the styles closely relate to the communication style of the individuals who fall into that group.

*On the next page is a communication analysis. Please circle the letter beside the statement in each question that reflects your first choice for each question.*

## A Communication Analysis

1.  What is your preferred way of dressing?

    (E)    *Designer, classy, more formal.*

    (P)    *Bold colors, trendy, informal, lots of blacks.*

    (D)    *Gentle muted colors, casual, loose sweaters, tracksuits.*

    (O)    *Conservative classic, practical, business-like.*

2.  In meetings you are:

    (E)    *Direct and to the point, start on time, end quickly.*

    (P)    *Engaged, animated, excitable, friendly.*

    (D)    *Pleasant, peace-maker, casual.*

    (O)    *Specific, concise, accurate.*

3.  Which of the following would be your preferred shape?

    (E)    *Triangle.*

    (P)    *Squiggle.*

    (D)    *Circle.*

    (O)    *Square.*

4.  When making critical decisions, you require:

    (E)    *Options.*

    (P)    *Testimonials.*

    (D)    *Assurances.*

    (O)    *Evidence and proof.*

5.  If given free choice, where would you most prefer to live?

    *(E)*   Suburban palace, 2-story, 4-bedroom, paved driveway.

    *(P)*   Country home on acreage with friendly neighbors.

    *(D)*   Cabin on the lake, tranquility, family is accessible.

    *(O)*   Condo, townhouse, downtown area, social events.

6.  Your most favored vacation would be?

    *(E)*   Adventures and travel, with action and activities.

    *(P)*   Caribbean resort – sun, sand, lounging, parties.

    *(D)*   At home or at a cottage, rest, reading, and friends.

    *(O)*   Organized city or country tour, make new friends.

7.  When attending a seminar, you would prefer.

    *(E)*   Practical information netted out, few workshops.

    *(P)*   Lots of fun learning, jokes, analogies.

    *(D)*   Comfortable, low-pressure environment, connecting
    with nice people, workshop environment.

    *(O)*   Logically laid out, unambiguous information,
    follow the agenda, well researched.

8.  Which of the following most motivates you?

    *(E)*   Seeing and achieving results.

    *(P)*   Recognition, applause, and self-actualization.

    *(D)*   Sincerity and trusting affiliation with others.

    *(O)*   Making steady progress towards an identified plan.

9.  Is your office more:

    *(E)*     Neat and organized, with an in-charge ambience.

    *(P)*     Disorganized with fun stuff, files in piles.

    *(D)*     Friendly, with comfortable chairs and personal pictures.

    *(O)*     Working environment, laid out practically, wall board.

10. You prefer to sleep:

    *(E)*     On your back, straight out, not cramped, one leg on top.

    *(P)*     In a cuddling or almost fetal position.

    *(D)*     On your side with your knees slightly bent.

    *(O)*     On your stomach with arms and one leg raised slightly.

11. Are you more:

    *(E)*     High-assertive but more reserved.

    *(P)*     High-assertive and very outgoing.

    *(D)*     Less-assertive but very outgoing.

    *(O)*     Less-assertive and slightly reserved.

12. An appropriate summary of who you are:
    *(not the role you play in your profession)*

    *(E)*     Netting out complex problems, making critical decisions,
    being bottom line oriented.

    *(P)*     Seeing the bigger picture, conceptualizing, using your
    intuition and being creative. Important to have fun in life.

    *(D)*     Interpersonal relationships, helping others get along,
    expressing feelings as comfortably as ideas, working in teams.

    *(O)*     Establishing standards, maintaining self-discipline,
    admiring others who maintain a sense of discipline
    and quality about their work.

What this survey is designed to do is determine your primary and secondary strengths in the area of communication. In this test, the letters are represented as follows:

| | | | | |
|---|---|---|---|---|
| (E) | = | Eagle | Quantity | _____ |
| (D) | = | Dove | Quantity | _____ |
| (P) | = | Peacock | Quantity | _____ |
| (O) | = | Owl | Quantity | _____ |

Count up your scores in each of the letters and order them from highest to lowest. This will give you an indication of your preferred and secondary ways of communicating. On the following pages, I will describe what this all means.

## Birds of a Feather

These birds have certain characteristics and behaviors that we associate with them. I find that in the communications process, people also exhibit similar characteristics that relate to each of these birds. The people to whom I assign each of the styles appear to share similar characteristics with the respective birds.

As I have discussed throughout this chapter, any successful relationship between two people in life, whether they are family members, friends, couples, or business partners, requires one key element: communication alignment. Although effective communication is a natural ability, it is like swimming. We are naturally born with this ability, but we still need coaching and to be taught techniques to become proficient. Although most people manage to function passably without formal communication training, they communicate at an effectiveness level far below their potential.

It is no secret that skillful communication can boost success and improve relationships. For example, marriage counselors find that couples who are effective communicators report happier relationships than couples who have not developed stronger skills.

There is no single ideal or effective way to communicate. Some successful communicators are serious while others use humor. Some are gregarious while others are quieter, and some are straightforward while others hint diplomatically. Communication is not just verbal; it also engages the visual and kinesthetic elements of our demeanor.

Miscommunication occurs frequently when facial expressions and body language are not in alignment with the verbal message. Even verbal communication creates confusion when localized expressions or words with double meanings are used. When the "receiver" is unsure of the message being relayed, the message can be misconstrued. Clarification is an extremely important element in effective communication.

Communication competence is the ability to get desired results from others in a manner that maintains the relationship on terms that are acceptable to everyone. With practice and training, even the most inept of us can learn to be more effective in our day-to-day communications with others.

*"What we've got here is a failure to communicate."*

- Cool Hand Luke

## In communication, who you are is what you were born.

I have always been intrigued by how similar many people are in their communications. Those who communicate in similar ways appear to make similar choices and live similar lifestyles. Conversely, there are also people who communicate very differently, and they make different choices.

Throughout my life, I have found that I am very comfortable communicating with some people, and not with others. The ones I seem to connect with have interests similar to mine. The ones I am not as comfortable with communicate the same way and have similar interests as each other. So, I decided to study this phenomenon.

What I discovered is that we are all made up of 12 genetic temperaments. These include:

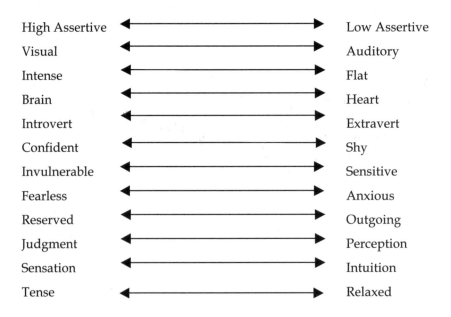

| High Assertive | ⟷ | Low Assertive |
| Visual | ⟷ | Auditory |
| Intense | ⟷ | Flat |
| Brain | ⟷ | Heart |
| Introvert | ⟷ | Extravert |
| Confident | ⟷ | Shy |
| Invulnerable | ⟷ | Sensitive |
| Fearless | ⟷ | Anxious |
| Reserved | ⟷ | Outgoing |
| Judgment | ⟷ | Perception |
| Sensation | ⟷ | Intuition |
| Tense | ⟷ | Relaxed |

It is how these genetic temperaments are aligned that makes the difference in how we like people to communicate with us. This alignment also determines many of our mannerisms. I should also say here that each of these genetic temperaments have been researched extensively.

### Bird Watching

Just as bird watchers delight in watching birds and their behaviors, you will enjoy watching for the "birds" (your friends, family, and professional acquaintances) I have described for you here.

### The Eagle

*"Just get 'er done!"*

Eagles can be quickly recognized by their very serious, concentrated, and stern look. They can stare at you for long periods of time without even blinking. They normally have short, neat hair. Their clothes are often tucked in, pressed and professional. They prefer pants with a crease. In fact, some female eagles actually buy slacks with a crease permanently sewn in them. They feel much better if their shoes have a great shine. When going through airports, they usually stop to have them polished. When standing in a relaxed position their arms are normally folded.

When answering the phone they will just say things like, "Bill here," or "This is Sam." Their answering machines are quick and to the point. When they leave messages for others they will just say, "This is Bill, call me."

Strengths associated with Eagles are: Their ability to make decisions, even critical ones, quite quickly and without stress. They can adapt quickly to change and like to take on new challenges. There is no obstacle that can't be overcome, and they usually remain focused on what they want and where they are going. They are goal-oriented, so everything they do is a means to an end. They are essentially practical, down-to-earth people who like to solve complex problems. Eagles see problems and opportunities as a challenge. Their philosophy is: "There is always a better way," and, "If it works, do it."

Some weaknesses include: Eagles often put results ahead of other people's feelings, and they always seem to be in a hurry. They are not very patient and will cut you off if you do not get to the point very quickly. They will often give you an answer before you have even finished asking your question. They might become pre-occupied with other matters if you start rambling during a conversation. They are especially impatient with touchy-feely discussions and discussions that do not come to a rapid conclusion. They sometimes appear to push people around, are regarded as poor listeners, and certainly do not like working in teams, unless they are in charge. Do not expect them to express personal feelings if you do not know them well.

When asked to choose between four shapes (circle, triangle, squiggle or square), the Eagle would normally select the triangle. It has been said that people who chose the triangle tend to be pre-occupied with sexual thoughts and see themselves as great lovers. Sigmund Freud, for example, makes reference to the triangle as being a phallic symbol, representing the sexual organs of the male and female. It is a pointed wedge-shape, which can push further and release greater energy than any other form. It has been said that the sexual instinct is the most powerful driver of motivation. However, it can also cause unhealthy behaviors and tense relationships if this energy is not released.

Aggressiveness is closely identified with the sex urge, since they both produce a high degree of excitation and seek active outlets for this energy. So, if a person is not able to satisfy one of these urges, they will replace it with the other.

In a study completed at the Yale University Child Development Clinic, researchers observed that drawing the triangle symbol required a more developed connection between the brain and hand. Most children did not draw this form until the age of five, though the circle and square were accomplished at three and four years of age.

Children who are Eagles tend to be aggressive, energetic and need to be in control. In drawings, they might depict steeples, airplanes and sailboats. Their doodling would contain many pointy figures. Even their handwriting will be pressed firmly into the paper, with strong points in it.

Eagles are sharp, independent thinkers and have a keen perception. They arrive at solutions quickly. They have the ability to work independently, and that's what they enjoy: they resist being placed in any subordinate position. Eagles can be emotional, but are not sensitive or compassionate to the emotional needs of others. Most people like and admire Eagles from a distance, but are apprehensive about approaching them on an intimate basis.

Eagles like to learn by trying out ideas, theories, and techniques to see if they work in practice. They visualize new ideas and look for opportunities to try them out. They are the type of people who return from conferences and workshops excited about new ideas they want to try out right away. Eagles like to get on with things and act quickly and confidently on any idea that sparks their interest.

When sleeping, Eagles like to lie straight out on their backs, taking up lots of space. They do not like being cramped. Often, they will stick just one leg out from under the blankets and put it on top. They prefer to live in the typical suburban palace: a two-story, four-bedroom house with a formal dining area and a paved circular driveway, a larger power-type vehicle, and lawn sprinklers. When entertaining, they are likely to plan the event well in advance to ensure that it goes smoothly.

For vacations, they like adventure and action. Whether it is camping in the wilderness, hiking, fishing, skiing, golf, or even white water rafting, they like to be active and not sit around and waste a vacation doing nothing.

Eagles' offices are often neat and organized. They display their qualifications, trophies, and certificates of achievement. If possible, they have their large power furniture arranged in an "I'm in charge here" layout with their desk facing the door.

Some well-known Eagle politicians are: Margaret Thatcher, Ross Perot, Jean Chretien, Winston Churchill, and Vladimir Putin.

Each of us has both a primary and secondary style of receiving communication. If we can recognize that, we can possibly increase our effectiveness by as much as 75%. The three Eagle-dominant styles are as follows.

## Eagle-Doves

Eagle-Dove combinations are self-motivated individuals with an inexhaustible supply of energy, which constantly needs to be released. People are important to Eagle-Doves. Their need to give love is greater than their need to receive it. In relationships with others, they become more the giver than the taker.

They want to take action quickly and will not wait around for somebody else to make a move or to come up with an idea. They enjoy competition and challenges and they do not discourage easily.

Eagle-Doves have quick minds and frequently act on impulse and intuition. Projects that tend to go on for a long time begin to bore Eagles-Doves, since they constantly like new challenges.

Sometimes they can be understanding and compassionate, but these feelings are often overruled by their impatient urge to get on with the job. One problem with this combination is that they develop internal stress, since, on one hand they are sensitive to others' feelings, but on the other hand, they just want to get on with it and will walk over people to get to where they want to go. They will then feel bad about what they did.

Individuals with the Eagle-Dove combination and a strong Peacock influence are highly energetic and are more imaginative. They come up with different approaches to achieve what they want.

They tend to be easily upset when others do not treat them fairly, and tend to lose their temper quickly. However, they will just as quickly forgive and become friends again.

## Eagle-Owls

Eagle-Owl individuals are more left-brain and are not into self-appreciation. However, they are much easier people to live with. Their aggressive energy goes into constructive outlets that depend more upon their skills and abilities than being emotionally fed by others.

They are able to perceive a situation quickly, evaluate it using reason and logic, and make the decisions necessary to resolve it. They normally do not allow emotions to interfere with reason. They are very realistic, with both feet on the ground, and do not waste time fantasizing or daydreaming.

Eagle-Owl combinations with an additional dove influence are able to experience more creative thought. They will occasionally find the time to look for romance and idealism in the things they do.

## Eagle-Peacocks

When communicating with Eagle-Peacocks, you must get to the facts very quickly and not waste their time. You must be very personable and show them that you also appreciate fun in life and even fit a joke into the conversation.

They are highly independent and individualistic people. They have great imagination and possess high aggressive energy that gives them unlimited scope for expression. They generate great amounts of mental activity that requires creative outlets.

They will not be controlled by conventionalism, tradition, or socially acceptable norms. Even though they like to be in the company of others, they find they must be in control and are most productive and creative when in seclusion.

They can be stimulated both by facts and imagination and will use this combination to artistically express themselves.

Eagle-Peacocks have a great desire to leave their mark on the universe and contribute to improving society in some way. However, they also want the recognition for doing this before they die.

If Eagle-Peacocks have an additional Owl trait, they feel a greater need to be secure in actual living situations. Because of this they are more likely to conform and live by the rules of the society. If their third style is Dove, they want to be very sensitive to others, but at the same time will not let anyone get in the way of their goals. They have a need to connect and be close to others, but usually end up with only a few close friends.

## Peacocks

*"Are we having fun yet?"*

Peacocks can be recognized by their bright clothes and big friendly grins, and usually have a twinkle in their eyes that makes people wonder what they are up to or what mischievous thoughts they are having. Some people have a bad hair day; Peacocks have bad hair lives. No matter what they do, they never seem to be satisfied with how their hair turns out.

Men, when they were teenagers, would grow it long, shave it off, would part it on the right, then on the left. Teenage girls always cry after having their hair cut. Women will go to a hairdresser, spend a lot of money on a new style, and immediately go straight home to the sink and wash it out.

Peacocks like their clothes to be trendy, unique, and fashionable. Although they are attracted to brightly colored clothes, if you go into the closet of a Peacock, you will find mostly black. Another shopping tendency the Peacocks have is, if they purchase something they really like, they will immediately go back and buy another one exactly the same. They will keep the second one to start wearing at a later date.

When answering the phone, their voice and words are optimistic and cheerful. When you ask, "How are you?" they will always answer "Great," "Wonderful," "Sensational," or some other lively response. They usually sound truly pleased to talk with you. Their offices are usually cluttered. They have toys and cartoons. Much of the time they have files sitting around in piles. Once in a while they make an effort to clean it up, but to no avail—it just ends up back the way it was.

In their natural state, Peacocks are outgoing, spontaneous, and highly expressive. Although they are very enthusiastic, they react quickly to any perceived threat. Their main mission in life is to have fun. They are people with great imaginations, can be very creative, and behave optimistically in most situations. Their imaginations are stimulated by an intense desire to see and know more. They do not generally accept the status quo, and like to go off on adventures in search of new discoveries. They get along well with people and have a charisma that attracts others to them instantly. They are never at a loss for words in a social situation.

Peacocks tackle problems by brainstorming. As soon as the excitement from one activity has died down, they are busy looking for the next. They tend to thrive on the challenge of new experiences, but are bored with implementation and longer-term consolidation. They are gregarious people, constantly involving themselves with others, but in doing so they tend to put themselves at the center of all activity.

In their negative state, they tend to interrupt you when speaking, exaggerate, and if they listen at all, it is only to see when you are going to stop talking so they know when to start. They are poor time managers and often arrive at meetings late. They like new projects but become bored quickly and go looking for something else. They do not like detailed work and may not follow through on important items, which causes them problems with their work.

Sometimes they are not in touch with reality. Much of their thinking time is spent in higher thought beyond the boring existence of everyday living. They can be aggressive, especially if they have a strong Eagle presence. When a Peacock's natural ability to be imaginative is suppressed, there will probably be negative consequences for the person who gets in his or her way.

Peacocks must channel their energy into constructive activity. If this does not happen, they may become withdrawn or aggressive. They always seem to be searching for excitement, and to others may not always appear to have two feet firmly on the ground.

The symbol that tends to attract them first is the squiggle – the symbol of imagination and creativity. Peacocks are very creative people and express that when they are totally in their zone. This is even apparent in their handwriting, which is hard to read and tends to go off the line. They bring their creativity and open-mindedness to all aspects of their lives. Many of their ideas could never be implemented, but they are fascinating to listen to.

Peacocks prefer to sleep in a fetal position, and they like to cuddle, whether it is with people, pillows, or pets. They would prefer to live in a country home with acreage, perhaps own horses or other animals, and spend leisure time visiting and joking with friendly neighbors.

For vacations, they like to get away to a Caribbean beach resort and spend most of their time in the sun, resting, relaxing, and talking to people at the swim-up pool bar.

In the learning process, Peacocks involve themselves fully and without reservation in new experiences. They enjoy the here and now and are happy to be dominated by immediate experiences. They are open-minded, not skeptical, and this tends to make them enthusiastic about anything new. Their philosophy is: "I'll try anything once." They tend to act first and consider the consequences later. Their days are filled with activity.

Well-known political Peacocks include: Ronald Reagan, Pierre Trudeau, Tony Blair, Vincente Fox, Rt. Hon. Michaëlle Jean, and Nicolas Sarkozy.


### Peacock-Doves

The Peacock-Dove combination is sensitive and ideal-istic, always looking for beauty and romance at every opportunity. Peacock-Doves search for an ideal love that will go beyond the normal relationship. They can often be found alone in thought. They like the warmth and security of being with people. The greatest pleasure they experience is their love for other human beings.

Friends seldom live up to the ideal image Peacock-Doves have of people; thus they become disappointed in relationships. They can be warm and responsive to people who accept them as individuals and who recognize the creative people they are. Although sensitive and idealistic, when threatened by an outside force or person, they can become aggressive. They will defend a principle to the end even if their security is in danger.

## Peacock-Owls

When communicating with Peacock-Owls make sure that, after your initial friendliness, you follow up with accurate and appropriate facts and details. These people are both dreamers and realistic at the same time. They will ponder into their imagination and then wake up to the safer practicalities of the real world. Their openness to new ideas and willingness to see and accept change can work positively in developing an inherent ability to adjust to change.

Since their need for security is also very strong, they try to keep both feet on the ground consistently enough to function as a member of the social environment. Home may be important, but variety and change is needed to keep them excited. If strong Eagle tendencies are present, Peacock-Owls could become hostile and foster resentment, especially when they are interrupted or held back. They are more involved with themselves rather than with other people. Personal relationships might take a backseat to other interests. Even family is more a means of securing their need for home stability than for exchanging a personal love. Other people or emotional attachments do not usually influence them.

This is the other group of people who often feel self-imposed internal stress, because the Owl tendency is to check everything multiple times before proceeding. The Peacock operates by "ready-shoot-aim." Inevitably some things will not be perfect, and that will cause the Owl in them to not sleep at night worrying about it.

## Peacock-Eagles

The Peacock-Eagle is a dynamic individual who possesses all the qualities for success and leadership. Peacock-Eagles' minds are never at rest, and they can never seem to stop thinking and planning. They take laptop computers on vacation because their minds are in high gear all the time.

They have an ability to conceptualize, and bring abstract ideas into focus with accurate comprehension, which usually results in solid theories. They can absorb knowledge and understand abstract concepts without working at it too hard. They are great at developing solutions, but do not expect them to be around when it comes to actually implementing the solutions. They expect others to follow through with details of their projects because they become bored with follow-up and detailed procedures.

Challenges are a source of stimulation and pleasure. Peacock-Eagles search for a variety of areas to discharge their mental energies, which are continuously building up as they are being released. Although receptive to new ideas, they will not be led down the garden path by ideas that do not conform to some sort of intelligent order.

In relationships, Peacock-Eagles are either envied or idolized. Unfortunately, they do not make the ideal companion or mate, because they spend little time developing interpersonal relationships, and are quite intolerant of weaknesses in others. They have a strong need for companionship, consciously or unconsciously finding relationships with people who have similar values.

Security is not a strong motivator for Peacock-Eagles, and they are unable to truly relax and enjoy others people's company. They resist social situations and shy away from being part of a group. Very little of their free time is devoted to parties or play, and even humor must be sprinkled with provocative thought to be appealing. Those with a strong Owl influence are even less motivated to develop strong relationships and have little compassion and patience with others. They do not suffer fools.

## The Dove

*"Let's all just get along!"*

Doves can be spotted by their sincere, friendly smiles, their warm eyes, untucked clothing and relaxed postures. One of the first things you will notice about Doves is their heads are cocked just slightly off to the left or right. They have a more relaxed handshake, and they buy shoes for comfort rather than style. Doves are very much into tranquility and pursue it in all areas of their lives.

Their handwriting tends to be rounded, with emphasis on a circular motion as well as curls at the end of words. Their voicemail usually says something like, "Good morning, this is Sally, I'm sorry I am not here to take you call.

Your call is very important to me. Please leave your name and number and I will be sure to get back to you as soon as I can."

The symbol Doves are most often drawn to is the circle, which is the symbol of peace, love and harmony. Think of all the pleasurable items that are round, soft and warm. For children, it is a rattle, a ball, or a mother's warm breasts, which are a comfort and delight. There are no sharp edges to hurt them. Children respond to round, smooth objects, which soothe, pacify, and provide safe play. This is reflected in Doves' behavior. They do not like violence, will run away from a fight, shrink at the sight of an accident, and find tense arguments distressing. Doves mostly seek affection and approval, which they find in non-threatening situations. They tend not to be hostile or aggressive and would rather play than fight. Doves do have a tendency to be possessive and jealous about people who are close to them and things that bring them personal pleasure.

Doves tend to sleep on their sides in the "spoon" position. They would prefer the tranquility of living in a cabin in the woods and enjoy their solitude. They take pleasure in watching sunsets, relaxing, floating around in a paddle-boat, and having their family and close friends accessible when necessary.

They often prefer a vacation at someone's home or cottage where they can sleep in, catch up on their reading, and see some friends and visit family. At work, even their office has a friendly atmosphere to it, decorated with pictures and comfortable chairs. When co-workers come to them for favors, they have a hard time saying no, and are often taken advantage of.

Doves are warm, friendly people who listen actively and are very patient. They value personal relationships above all, work cohesively with others, and are articulate and orga-nized. They prefer to work with others who get along. You can always count on Doves when they give you their word. They have good counseling skills and are usually known around the office as peacemakers because they like to help others. Doves tend to adopt a low profile and have a quiet, tolerant, relaxed air about them.

Doves are very trusting, often feel let down by other people, and worry too much about what others think. Other people sometimes see their friendly and accommodat-ing nature as a weakness and will try to take advantage of that loyalty. Doves tend to spend too much personal time doing things for others. They do not like traumatic change that they have not had time to get used to and accept, and they are reluctant to take risks, and avoid conflict at all costs. They do not react quickly when confronted. However, they will hold a grudge against people who have done them wrong.

When learning, Doves like to stand back to ponder expe-riences and observe from many different perspectives, considering all possible angles and implications before mak-ing a move. They prefer to take a back seat in meetings and discussions. They enjoy observing other people in action. They listen to others and get the drift of the discussion be-fore making their own points. They do not always push for what they want. When making a decision, they tend to post-pone reaching and announcing definitive conclusions for as long as possible. They solicit input from as many people they can and prefer to think about it thoroughly before com-ing to any conclusion. They often know what the decision is going to be, but input from others helps confirm what they already know. When they react, they consider the whole picture, which includes the sum total of all their experiences and observations.

Political Dove figures include Bill Clinton, Jean Charest, and Nelson Mandela.

## Dove-Owls

Dove-Owls who have Eagle strengths are motivated most by love and the desire to share pleasures with others. They then seek to secure this love by building a circle of home, family, and friends. They do not wish anything to interfere with or disturb the lifestyle they have patterned, and feel threatened by unpredicted or unnecessary changes.

Those with strong Peacock characteristics are motivated by love and the desire to share pleasures. Their need for security is second only to wanting love and to be loved. They do not focus on their goals or ambitions except their desire for family comfort and home living. They have a strong capacity for pleasure, with an added touch of imagination, and they can make many people very happy.

## Dove-Peacocks

Dove-Peacocks are romantic idealists. They search for a profound love with another individual to satisfy their every emotion and desire. Wealth and social success are of less concern since they are interested in attaining loftier goals to satisfy their needs. To be successful, they must have someone who they can trust, who will represent them and protect them. They are extremely imaginative and will un-consciously invent an unreal image of others. This results in possible disillusions and disappointments.

Dove-Peacocks with strong Owl attributes are realists with both feet on the ground. They prefer to accept and move on solid and sound ideas, rather than reach for the unreachable. They have two extremes to their nature. They are playful and compassionate, and enjoy the pleasure of being with people, but they also feel an aggressive drive to get ahead without the interference of emotional feelings. Unfortunately, these two extremes could ultimately come together and conceal their inner feelings.

Dove-Peacocks with additional Eagle influence are more aggressive in their search for romance and more ambitious in finding outlets for their creative abilities. They stand up to other people who threaten their ideals and principles and will fight for the principle of personal rights.

### Dove-Eagles

Dove-Eagles are not concerned with financial security. These people are not afraid to face problems and try to resolve them. Freedom always comes before safety. For them, the best security is the freedom to express their feelings and abilities.

They have internal strength because the Dove makes them sensitive to others, but when the Eagle in them takes over, they will walk over anyone in their way. Then they will feel badly because they hurt someone else's feelings.

Dove-Eagles with Peacock tendencies are motivated by the desire for love, which is also a major factor behind their sexual motivation and drive for success. They might have a touch of romanticism and frequent fantasies.

### The Owl

*"We don't want any surprises here."*

Owls can be recognized by their cross look. In fact, people often ask them, "Are you mad at me for some reason? Have I done something wrong?" Children who are owls often pout if things are not going their way. Owls' hair and clothes are practical and they normally check the weather or the day's agenda before getting dressed.

Many Owls have trouble looking people directly in the eyes for a period of time without looking away or moving back. As adults, a higher proportion of them wear glasses.

Their voicemail usually says something like: "Good morning, this is Tuesday, May 2nd. I will be out of my office attending a meeting until 11:00AM. Please leave your name, number, time of your call and the reason," etc. When standing in conversation with someone, they normally like to lean against a wall or post.

Their primary symbol choice is the square, which reflects a strong desire for security. The squareness often appears in their handwriting, as well. This shape came into their lives the first time they were placed in a crib as an infant. It kept them safe and secure. They liked to play with blocks, and as their intelligence developed, they placed one on top of the other, building structures.

Because of their focus on security, their home is their castle. Whether it is gardening, taking care of repairs and improvements, entertaining in the home, or generally puttering around, they are comfortable and content in a home situation. They like working with their hands and like to build things. Their gift of patience helps them to follow through each step of a project until it's completed with accuracy. When this is carried to an extreme, it will cause them to develop perfectionist or conventionalist behaviors later in life.

Owls are both logical and practical, accumulating information that can be useful. Abstract thinking does not come naturally to them, and they do not indulge in romantic and idealistic philosophies. Owls often have RRSPs for themselves as soon as they start work and RESPs for their children when they are born. Sometimes they actually purchase a home before they get married and pay off the mortgage prior to having children.

Owls learn by adapting and integrating what is being communicated into complex but logically sound theories. They think problems through in a step-by-step, pragmatic manner. They tend to come across as perfectionists who will not rest easily until things are tidy and fit into a rational scheme.

Owls are interested in basic assumptions, principles, theories, models and systems. Their philosophy is: "If it is logical, it is right." They frequently ask questions like, "Does this make sense?" and "How does this fit with that?"

Owls are detached, analytical, and dedicated to objectivity rather than anything subjective or ambiguous. Their approach to problems is consistently logical. This is their mindset, and they rigidly reject anything that does not fit with it.

When sleeping, Owls like to lie on their stomachs with their arms up by their head. They tend to gravitate to a lifestyle of Condo living in an urban setting where they can eat out, travel, and attend theatre, musicals and social events.

They usually plan their vacations well in advance and select organized tours of cities and countries. They visit museums, galleries, cafes, concerts, and shopping areas with the hope of learning of new things.

Their offices have an air of conservatism and all the tools for working such as a clock, wall-chart, white board, graphs, barometer, or, at the very least, a desk organizer. They adhere to their to-do lists religiously and usually have one for work, one for home, and sometimes others.

Owls are logical, very self-disciplined, and can assimilate information accurately. They focus on quality and admire people with high standards regarding work and life. Their opinions are well thought-out, and they make decisions primarily based on facts. They have a knack for problem solving and manage their time well. They are analytical, patient, and come across as calm and rational even though internally they may not be. They prefer a task-oriented environment and pride themselves on being precise and accurate. They are most comfortable when there are rules or guidelines to follow.

Owl weaknesses include getting stuck in an "either/or" mindset, disliking emotional or sensitive situations, and coming across as impersonal even though they are very personable. They may lose sight of the "big picture." They avoid confrontation, taking risks, and making fast decisions. In critical situations, they put right vs. wrong ahead of other people's feelings. They tend not to be team players and become defensive when criticized. They have certain standards and strive to meet those whenever possible.

Some Owl political figures include Preston Manning, George Bush, Stephen Harper, Abraham Lincoln, Henry Kissinger, Richard Nixon, and Mother Teresa.

### Owl-Doves

Owl-Doves' view of love is that it belongs within the family unit, and even if it is lacking there, they will not compensate for it elsewhere. They like the comfort of culture and tradition, and enjoy friends and family. As peace-loving individuals, they dislike violence.

Owls-Doves can be counted on to be reasonable and logical in living situations, and will compromise in order to satisfy others. Their thoughts and actions are based on what they believe is practical. They rarely act on emotion alone and quite often feel that they live a dull existence.

Owl-Doves with Eagle strengths like to feel safe and secure. When reaching for a goal, they make sure they can achieve it — otherwise they will not reach for it at all. Their homes and everything contained within are their most valued possessions. Whatever pleasure they might enjoy on the outside will be sacrificed if it jeopardizes the stability and security of home and family life.

When Owl-Doves have Peacock attributes, they tend to glamorize love interests and a home situation so that these objects become their source of pleasure and a means to satisfy their need for security. These people are even less ambitious and competitive, and will not struggle for fame or worldly gain beyond what is required for comfortable living. They enjoy simple pleasures and find that their needs are easily accessible.

### Owl-Eagles

Owl-Eagles believe in authority and discipline in both the home and in business, and are not easily swayed by emotion or hard-luck stories. They do not spend much time dreaming or fantasizing.

Owl-Eagles with Dove tendencies will take aggressive action to ensure the security of self and family, and are willing to compete and fight for it. They are intelligent, and their approach to problems is both perceptive and logical. This causes them to act first on reason rather than emotion, making them winners more often than losers. They work hard to provide a good lifestyle for their families.

Those with Peacock strengths are more imaginative and will add a touch of creative thought to the things in which they participate.

They are serious-minded, intent upon keeping emotions under control. They do not need to have their ego stroked by others, and will seek security and self-actualization from personal accomplishments.

## Owl-Peacocks

Owl-Peacocks are not easy people to understand or to live with, for there are two strongly opposing factors guiding them. On one hand, they respond to practical reasoning and logic. On the other hand, their urge for an exciting and romantic life is strong, which causes them internal conflict and stress.

Living a routine existence creates great frustration, and they might rebel against the lack of change in their lives. But, they are not always aggressive enough to make these changes in their own lives. These are the type of people who want to purchase a new home, but cannot make the decision to sell their old one or put in an offer on the new one. Recognition from friends and family and personal creative achievements offer some measure of satisfaction.

Owl-Peacocks are not interested in developing close relationships with other people because that is not a source of pleasure for them. Owl-Peacocks admire others who demonstrate high values, and they would like to be able to balance the real world and their dreams.

Frank Lloyd Wright was an architect with imagination and intense drive. He was an Owl-Peacock with an Eagle's drive. People like this have ideas that are constructed on a solid base, and though imagination may sweep them away on wild tangents, their ability to perceive a problem allows for using imaginative thought to a practical end.

## Summary of The Birds©

Once you have learned the strengths and weakness of each of these birds, and how to instantly recognize them, it will be much easier for you to adapt your communication style to be more effective when dealing with them. Understanding these differences will also mean that from now on there may not be anyone you meet who you will not like. You will just understand they have different needs.

This will also enable you to understand how people may behave at work and at social functions, how they approach risk-taking, how they will likely respond to certain stresses, how to approach them in a sales or even relationship situation, and how to deal with them as customers.

On the following page is a summary of the traits you should watch for. But remember, no one item should be used when making an overall determination since a person's secondary style may be predominant for some of the factors. The combination of different factors will be more accurate.

*Communication is all about understanding and being understood. Understanding the nature of these birds will provide the insights required so you can make yourself understood by others.*

| | EAGLE | PEACOCK | DOVE | OWL |
|---|---|---|---|---|
| **HAIR** | short/neat | never happy | basic | irrelevant |
| **FACE** | stern | grin | pleasant | cross |
| **EYES** | stare | twinkle | friendly | averted |
| **STANCE** | arms folded | pockets | head cocked | leaning |
| **CLOTHES** | tucked-in | black | loose | practical |
| **SHOES** | polished | fashionable | comfortable | utility |
| **STYLE** | designer | trendy | relaxed | conservative |

## General Bird Descriptions

It is important to know that in all my research, I have not found any correlations with regards to successful people, failures, gender, age, horoscopes, culture, criminals, musicians, leaders, kindness, mean spirited people, or even a predisposition towards certain occupations. I also want to repeat that this is not a study of personality styles. It is limited to how our genetic temperaments determine how we look, how we like to be communicated with, and many of the choices we make in life.

To illustrate this, in addition to the political figures noted previously, here are some samples of well-known personalities:

### World Leaders

| | |
|---|---|
| Eagle | Margaret Thatcher |
| Owl | Abraham Lincoln |
| Peacock | Tony Blair |
| Dove | Bill Clinton |

## Politicians

| | |
|---|---|
| Eagle | Hillary Clinton |
| Owl | Ruth Ginsberg |
| Peacock | Sarah Palin |
| Dove | Barbara Bush |

## Business Leaders

| | |
|---|---|
| Eagle | Madeleine Albright |
| Owl | Bill Gates |
| Peacock | Donald Trump |
| Dove | Walt Disney |

## Comedians

| | |
|---|---|
| Eagle | Don Rickels |
| Owl | Bob Newhart |
| Peacock | Tina Fey |
| Dove | Bill Cosby |

## Criminals

| | |
|---|---|
| Eagle | Ted Bundy |
| Owl | Ted Kaczynski |
| Peacock | Charles Manson |
| Dove | John Wayne Gacy, Jr. |

## Musicians

| | |
|---|---|
| Eagle | Tom Jones |
| Owl | Ringo Starr |
| Peacock | Elton John |
| Dove | John Lennon |

## American Idol Winners

| | |
|---|---|
| Eagle | Kris Allen |
| Owl | Lee Dewyze |
| Peacock | Adam Lambert |
| Dove | Rubin Stoddard |

## Talk Show Hosts

| | |
|---|---|
| Eagle | David Letterman |
| Owl | Larry King |
| Peacock | Oprah |
| Dove | Jay Leno |

While writing this book, I actually came across another piece of research on criminals that the FBI is currently conducting. Over the past 25 years, the FBI have been developing a motive-based profiling system by studying serial killers' behavior, character, methods, and signature at the crime scene. This system was originally created by a homicide detective and criminal psychologists (Richard Walter and Bob Keppel).

The profile is focused around four categories that are based on earlier studies of rapists. These are as follows:

### Power-Assertive Killer

They thrive on controlling their victims and asserting power over them. We are in the process of further investigatons. However, at this time I would say these may be the Eagles. Remember, the aggressive Eagle has a high need for power and control.

### Anger-Excitation Killer

These killers derive sadistic pleasure from inflicting pain and fear on their victims. These could be the Peacocks. Remember, Peacocks usually have quick tempers and will react with their emotion first.

### Anger-Retaliatory Killer

These killers attack their victims in revenge for a past offense, real or imagined. Remember the Doves—they do not get mad; they get even.

### Power-Reassurance Killer

They thrive on the fantasy of "seducing" and conquering their victims. I think these may align with the profile of the Owl. Remember, Owls are more reserved and introverted. This would be a way of expressing themselves with much fanfare. However, I will say it again, there is still more research to be done in this area.

### There Are No Correlations

Every once in a while, I hear someone say, "Oh, I bet accountants would be Owls," or, "Comedians would be Peacocks." Nope, I have found nothing to substance this. Certain businesses, however, can develop communication cultures. For instance, a company like IBM might have an Eagle culture, a chartered accounting firm might have an Owl culture, Child Welfare or Social Services might have a Dove culture, or an advertising firm might have a Peacock communication culture. However, if you assess each individual within those organizations, the communication types will be pretty much evenly distributed all the way around. Organizational communication culture is created by the industry they are in or the most influential leaders at the top.

Even countries develop communication cultures. For instance, the United States might be an Eagle. Brazil might be a Peacock. Perhaps Japan is an Owl, and Canada, of course, is a Dove. However, within each of these countries, individuals' communication types are basically equal all the way around, although the personality of a Brazilian Peacock is a lot different than the personality of a German Peacock.

Another thing that is said to me sometimes is: "Well I don't think we should be categorizing and pigeonholing people." But this is not pigeonholing people. Think of these communication types as four different languages. For instance, if you could speak English, French, Spanish, and Chinese, could you not be more successful and appeal to more people in the world? This theory works the same way. It is not about pigeonholing people, it is about understanding what others need in the communication process and modifying your language accordingly.

## To Be a More Effective Communicator

When you are communicating with Eagles, be brief, direct, and stick to business—they like their information presented to them bottom-lined and netted out. Focus on *what* you want, not *how* you want it. Let them share ideas and be in charge. They like getting results quickly, so be sure to provide incentives and recognition for fast action. Do not waste their time with details, because they grasp broad concepts quickly and will quickly turn off.

To win over a Peacock, right from the start you must be stimulating, conversational and witty. Smile, use analogies, and put him or her as the most important person in the interaction—Peacocks thrive on public recognition. Give Peacocks the opportunity to verbalize their ideas and visions. Unless they get this opportunity, they will not be open to listening to yours. When selling an idea to Peacocks, be sure to use testimonials and perceptions. Spin it so they will be recognized for their great insights and perceptions. The best way to engage a Peacock is to take him or her to lunch. Finally, remember they are not detail-oriented, so limit details in writing.

For the Doves, you must come across as sincere, personal, calm, agreeable, and supportive. Do not come on too strongly—they will see that behavior as similar to a used car salesman and back off. Be sure to focus on *what* you want and *how* you want it. Present changes in a non-threatening manner. Let them know you will minimize risks and then provide them a plan for support and reassurance. Be sure to clearly define roles and goals. Then be patient and give them time to think, adjust their views and beliefs, and respond. If you can make a personal connection with someone they know and trust, they will more likely listen to you and absorb what it is you are saying.

If you want to appear credible to an owl, be thoroughly prepared, objective, and persistent when presenting an idea. Provide lots of accurate detail in a relaxed manner. Focus on *what* you want, *why* you want it, and *when* you want it. Be sure to support everything with accurate data that you can substantiate. Prior to concluding a conversation, you should check for clarity of understanding. It is important that you are patient and allow for criticisms and changes. Owls feel this is their duty. They also want to be reassured that no surprises will occur.

### What should I do now?

To increase your own potential, here is what each of the Birds should do:

*If you are an Eagle* you should learn to listen more. Do not interrupt people who do not get to the point as quickly as you would like. Wait for the other person to finish asking their question before responding. Do not feel that you need to always pressure others to get them to perform. People work best at their own speed.

You have a natural competitive instinct. Try to curb that in situations where it is not required. Do not feel you have to take on an extraordinary amount of responsibility to appear valued. When connecting with others, be more personable and less task-oriented.

On a personal level, be more patient and tolerant of others' shortcomings and try to reduce your need to be in control. Although it not your intention, be less condescending to others who do not always see things your way.

*If you are a Peacock*, curb your desire to always be the centre of attention. Learn to talk less, and sincerely listen to the message that others are sharing. It is not necessary for you to dominate all conversations, and be in the limelight.

Don't intimidate others with your "larger than life" personality. Avoid coming on too strong with people you have just met. When trying to persuade others, state your case objectively.

A big weakness is your natural ability to see the big picture, often overlooking important details. Develop systems for follow up, appointments, meetings, and finances.

Not everything is life shattering; try to avoid public and dramatic overreactions. And finally, get down to business more quickly and do not always turn everything into a social event.

*If you are a Dove*, practice being more assertive. Before you are about to convey a message, organize your thoughts so you can get to the point more quickly. It is not always necessary to spare other people's feelings.

When the process of life is happening to your friends, don't always get personally involved. You spend more of your time trying to please others than you do yourself — stop it!

It is important that you do not get flustered under pressure. When a crisis comes along, initiate and take action. Do not always wait for everyone to be on board. And finally, set deadlines for your staff and ensure they stick to them.

*If you are an Owl:* you are highly intelligent, but not everything can be solved with pure facts. Trust your intuition more. When dealing with others, be more flexible and do not always appear so judgmental.

A weakness of many Owls is their desire for perfection — relax. That does not mean you have to accept sloppy work, but if mistakes do happen, or something is not perfect, don't lose sleep over it. Perfectionism is an extremely high cause of self-imposed internal stress.

Unlike the Peacocks, your strength is detail. However, sometimes that can lead to delayed action or even inaction. Learn to make decisions more quickly — you may never have all the facts you want to make that perfect decision.

In terms of people, be more spontaneous and give people more praise — if not for results, then for the effort shown. It will win you a lot more social capital.

I hope you will enjoy identifying these different Birds in your workplace and increasing the effectiveness of your communication on a more regular basis.

# iLeader Profile

## *Pat Minicucci*

*Pat Minicucci is the current Senior Vice President of the National Bank of Canada and currently oversees the Bank's operations outside Quebec. He joined Scotiabank in Montreal in 1997 and has held various positions in Retail Banking and Small Business Operations. Pat has held senior positions at the Montreal Trust Company and ScotiaBank, where he was in charge of their operations.*

Pat was one of four children from an immigrant family who took responsibility for his own success very early in life. However, going into business was not at the top of his mind. His initial desire was to become a doctor or an RCMP officer. However, because of his grades at the time and other matters, he was not able to pursue either of these options. He eventually achieved his B.Com at McGill and joined the Royal Bank, entering into their management training program. It was here he realized he had a talent for business and a natural ability for motivating people.

Pat was not only influenced by the good managers he had in his career, but also strongly influenced by the bad ones. In fact, it was from them he learned some of the best lessons, such as what not to do if you want to build a constructive team. He was fortunate to connect with a mentor, an older gentleman who he worked with on a board, and they subsequently became close friends. From his mentor, Pat learned that there is no one road to Rome, and that success comes to us via many alternatives. A person just has to remain open to explore all options.

Pat's real strength is his focus on building positive corporate communications. Even in large bureaucracies, it is important to keep people connected and be in constant communication with them. For years, he has maintained a process of sending out inspirational quotes and messages to all his staff. He lets each of them know that he personally cares and sincerely wants the best for them. He believes that each individual is important to the overall success of the corporate mission. His messages come from the heart, and his people know he genuinely cares.

A hard lesson Pat has had to learn along the way is that everyone is not like him. Others do not have the same work ethic, think the same, or place the same importance on the things he believes are critical. So becoming more patient and tolerant of others' differences and even their perceived shortcomings was a large part of his growth and maturing.

Pat has never believed that money was a motivator of higher performance. But, if people could believe in the organization's cause and understand its direction, they would become intrinsically motivated and produce the necessary results.

Pat's enduring quality that keeps him going no matter how tough things become is his emotional mindset of the "fear of failure." "For me, failure was just not an acceptable outcome in any situation," he says. Pat does not fail, but he also knows when to pull the plug on an initiative—when the law of diminishing returns is evident, or when continued, concentrated effort will result in a low ROI.

*Pat Minicucci has over 31 years of financial services experience and, prior to his appointment as head of the Caribbean Region for the National Bank of Canada, served in other capacities, including Senior Vice President. He was appointed to the Board of The Bank of Nova Scotia Jamaica Ltd. and the Scotia Group Jamaica Ltd. on November 26, 2007. He was also a Director of Scotiabank Trinidad & Tobago, Scotiabank Bahamas, and Maduro & Curiel's Bank. Pat is past President of the Canadian Italian Business Association of Montreal and the National Federation of Canadian Italian Business & Professional Association.*

# Summary

## *Chapter Four*

## Macro Communications in a Micro World

🌀 *Effective communication reduces stress.*
🌀 *The human function curve.*
🌀 *Understanding the message.*

## Listening Skills

🌀 *Listening is important.*
🌀 *Improving listening skills.*
🌀 *Listening for understanding.*

## Non Verbal Communication

🌀 *Interpreting the message.*
🌀 *Communication analysis.*
🌀 *The Birds©.*
🌀 *Increasing effectiveness.*

# Chapter Five

## *Creating the Culture*

*"Coming together is a beginning.*
*Keeping together is progress.*
*Working together is success."*

- Henry Ford

The power of a constructive working culture should never be underestimated. It will have profound and long lasting effects on business results and the morale of the staff and will give customers a stronger confidence in the organizations. iLeaders who are able to rise above the day-to-day operations and ongoing issues and focus on creating this will ensure sustainability in the future.

Culture is the most difficult of all organizational attributes to change, outlasting people, products, services, founders, leadership, and all other physical attributes of the organization. Where culture is strong, people do something because they believe it is the right thing to do. Organizational culture describes the psychology, attitudes, experiences, beliefs, and values (both personal and cultural) of an organization.

There is a direct link between organizational culture and performance effectiveness. The values of an organization must be more than just a poster on the wall. In order to create a culture of high trust where everyone communicates effectively, shares the vision, and is able to work unrestricted by bureaucracy and rules, the organization much reach the stage of empowerment. When this is achieved, morale is higher, people are more productive, customers are more satisfied, and management is less stressed.

*Empowerment is not about allowing people to make decisions. Empowerment is about allowing people to make mistakes.*

### Shared Values and Fundamental Beliefs

Culture is the most difficult of all organizational attributes to change, outlasting people, products, services, founders, leadership, and all other physical attributes of the organization.

In his book *Lessons from the Monkey King*, Arthur F. Carmazzi says there are common cultures present in organizations today. They are as follows:

### Brand Congruent Culture

This most often happens during the Entrepreneurial Phase. People in this culture believe in the product or service of the organization, feel good about what their company is trying to achieve, and cooperate to achieve it. They are passionate and seem to have similar goals in the organization. They use personal resources to actively solve problems and while they don't always accept the actions of management or others around them, they see their jobs as important. Most everyone in this culture is operating at the level of Group.

### The Blame Culture

This culture cultivates distrust and fear. People blame each other to avoid being reprimanded or put down. This results in no new ideas or personal initiative because people don't want to risk being wrong. This culture is often found during the bureaucratic phase.

### Multi-Directional Culture

This culture minimizes cross-department communication and cooperation, usually during the Silo Phase. Loyalty is only to specific groups (departments). Each department becomes a clique and is often critical of the other departments, which in turn creates lots of gossip. The lack of cooperation creates inefficiency in the organization.

### Live and Let Live Culture

This culture is complacency, which is found most often during the Matrix Phase. It manifests in mental stagnation and low creativity. People in this culture have little future vision and have given up their passions. There is average cooperation and communication, and things do work, but they do not grow. People have developed their personal relationships and decided who to stay away from; there is not much left to learn.

### Leadership Enriched Culture

People view the organization as an extension of themselves. They feel good about what they personally achieve through the organization and have exceptional cooperation. Individual goals are aligned with the goals of the organization, and people will do what it takes to make things happen. As a group, the organization is more like family providing personal fulfillment, which often transcends ego, so people are consistently bringing out the best in each other. In this culture, leaders do not develop followers, but develop other leaders. This is what happens when an organization is able to reach the Empowered Team Phase.

Carmazzi's model requires application of his Directive Communication psychology to evolve the culture. While the idea of having a leadership enriched organization is inspirational, it would require substantial leadership resources to develop. The concept of evolving the culture assumes two things. One, that the right people with the right skills have been hired, and two, that every individual in the organization wants to do a good job. After that, any behaviors that result in poor performance are usually manifestations of psychology that the group or organization has created through policies, leadership, and poor communication.

### A Case for Corporate Responsibility

I work with many executives who are sincerely trying to improve the environment of corporate responsibility. I also see an increased awareness on the part of consumers and investors who demand improved social responsibility on the part of the companies from which they buy and in which they invest.

Because of this, many organizations are developing their own "Codes of Conduct" and "Mission Statements", which encompass more than making a profit. But this is not enough. There must also be an effort to ensure all employees understand, and are committed to, this ethical way of doing business. As discussed earlier in the book, too many companies just write up a code of ethics, dump it on employees without their input or approval, and hope that something good will happen.

The other issue is that on one hand employees see posters on the walls advertising a wonderful code of conduct and see wonderful words in the annual report about how people-oriented and ethical the company is. However, if you talk to employees in many of these same organizations, they will not agree that they really mean it. If this is the case, the company will experience a group of employees who are cynical, sarcastic, and make snide remarks about the management initiative in the cafeteria. What I have discovered is that a company which has not taken the time to create a vision, mission, and values statement is better off than one which has done it but not implemented and cascaded it properly.

### Value Based Decision Making

There is a process to establishing or enhancing a culture. The first thing to do is to establish values. Once the values have been established in an organization, it is then important to educate all employees on how to make decisions within the boundaries of the value system. Creating a decision-making process allows employees to not just follow the rules blindly—which results in a phenomenon known as group think—but to make decisions which go outside of the rules without implicating the company.

> *"In today's organizations we need wild ducks,*
> *as long as they fly in formation."*
>
> - Tom Watson, Jr., IBM

### Is Organization Culture Important?

In his book *Leviathan*, Thomas Hobbes, wrote about a world without a code of ethics. He concluded that the result would be simple. There would be no farming because others would eat the farmers' food. There would be no building because others would take his house. There would be no music or art because people would only be concerned about their own survival.

What saves us from this type of world is our ability to create an ethical code by which we all agree to live. Hobbes called it a "social contract": I will respect you and yours, and you respect me and mine. What a great idea, but very difficult to enforce.

What's to stop someone from breaking the agreement and taking advantage of the situation? Laws and punishments have some effect, but the law cannot cover every situation and catch every violator. There has to be something more to hold the contract together.

Hobbes recognized that in order to exist as a society, we require a general, intrinsic desire to live cooperatively, so that we keep promises for the sake of keeping promises and abstain from violence because violence is undesirable. Compliance with a basic code of conduct needs to be in place, if we are to build a strong and viable society

Similarly, removing obstacles within the workplace, especially fear, is key to building a new culture. New leaders must be culture builders, providing direction and purpose. They must also encourage it by example. If you want to determine the culture of an organization, look at its last ten promotions to senior management. This says it all.

*How all managers behave must be a reflection of the core culture now desired by the organization.*

### Developing Values

When establishing values, an organization must consider the two or three fundamental beliefs that, when translated into behaviors, are critical to success. These are often a reflection of the internal culture and the past reputation and behavior of the organization. For an organization to have more than a few values would just not be manageable. Not only that, too many core values would cause some be in conflict with each other when people tried to apply them on a day-to-day, decision-making basis.

Not only should there be no more than three (absolute maximum four) values, but one must be careful about what they are. If a company has a value of "honesty", but managers aren't always open and truthful, or there is a value of "best customer service" yet managers reprimand employees for trying to provide just that, the company will end up with a work force that is cynical and will sneer behind the backs of the management team and actually laugh openly with each other at the posters on the wall.

Often I see companies put "Integrity" as one of their values. Integrity is NOT a value. Integrity is the adherence to what you believe or espouse. Prisons and the mafia are the places where the highest level of integrity is found. In those organizations, you live by the code, or die. Integrity is actually what makes all the other values work.

For an organization to be successful, it must position values as the foundation on which its vision, mission, and strategic objectives are created. As Ken Blanchard and Sheldon Bowles state in their inspiring book *Gung Ho!* "In a Gung Ho organization values are the real boss. Values are to guide your behavior…you have to ensure the organization is internally aligned — everyone singing from the same hymn book."

Once values are established, the organization must go through the process of ensuring that all employees understand and buy into these values. The biggest problem with achieving employee buy-in is credibility. They may see the values as a poster on the wall, but, if they do not observe executives modeling them appropriately, reinforcing them on a day-to-day basis, and being consistent with how violation is handled, the values will remain just that: posters on the wall. Unfortunately, if there is not a commitment to the values by all staff, everything the company wants to do will take a much stronger effort, and employees will appear to become high-maintenance.

There should be consequences in the form of reinforcement for appropriate behaviors and decisions that encourage these principles. Staff should also know up front that any conduct violation of this code could result in disciplinary action or termination of employment, even if the action did result in an increase in profit or revenue.

Organizational Values provide the framework within which employees must work. Personal Values provide the framework from which employees approach their work. They represent our character: who we really are. In order for people to be happy and successful in their careers, both need to be understood and acknowledged. If a person finds they are working in an organization whose business conduct is not in alignment with their own personal values, that person will never find happiness and true success in that organization.

### Defining Values

To consider values in the workplace is to probe the very reason people work and why they behave in the ways they do in their jobs. It is well known that our values are formed in the first five years of our lives. I also believe, based on studies, that a person's business values are formed in the first five years of his or her work-life.

Values give meaning to life and work and provide fulfillment. Your most basic fundamental beliefs are values. These are the principles that will arouse an emotional reaction if you perceive them to be threatened. Knowing the values that are most fundamental to you will enable you to make the best career choices. You spend more time at work than at any other single activity, including sleeping, so your profession has the greatest potential to satisfy your basic needs. Therefore, it is important that the place where you work has a code of conduct that is conducive to your own primary and personal values. If your organization's values are in alignment with your own personal values, you are more likely to find that what you do is meaningful, purposeful, and less stressful.

A country's laws usually represent the lowest common denominator of the values system of the culture. We should be careful not to be preoccupied with judging other people's (or cultures') values. We should only judge our own behaviors against the values that we espouse.

You are about to determine your critical values. The good news is there are lots to choose from. The bad news is you cannot maintain a primary focus on them all. If you would like to understand a little more about your own priority of values, complete the exercise on the following pages. Review values on page 265.

> *"Values are not just words values are what we live by.*
> *They're about the causes that we champion*
> *and the people we fight for."*
>
> - US Senator John Kerry

### Creating the Framework

The first step an organization must take is to decide upon, then articulate, its top three values. Then it must educate managers in the appropriate behaviors associated with these values. The next step is to prioritize them, because there will be times that decisions to be made will cause two or more values to conflict with each other. So all managers should know which value trumps the others.

If you can assess the value priority of potential employees, then you can create alignment between the natural decisions they will make and the culture of the organization.

Most managers in companies today do not know the difference or the definition of most of the terminology used in a culture. Simple definitions are as follows:

**Ethics**: a code of behavior that is acceptable to a culture or organization

**Integrity**: a measurement of the adherence to values. Integrity is not a value! Integrity is when what you feel and believe on the inside matches what you say and do on the outside. Integrity is what makes all your other values work.

**Scruples**: the restraining force that keeps you from violating the values you espouse.

**Morals**: an individual's own personal interpretation of each of the values they espouse.

**Corporate Culture**: the shared values and basic beliefs which determine the moral climate in an organization. Corporate credos are expressions of the values that the organization holds, and function as fundamental mission statements. They should not be just a set of rules or regulations,

**Deontology**: any theory based upon the categories of duty, responsibility, or obligation. The Deontologist holds that these are the defining characteristics of ethics such that an action is ethical if it fulfills one's duties, responsibilities or obligations; an action is not ethical if it neglects these basic beliefs.

**Teleology**: an ethical theory which holds that an action is ethical depending on the consequences it produces. The end justifies the means.

**Situational Ethics**: an ethical theory that holds that an action is right or wrong depending upon the context of its situation. (It all depends.)

**Code of Conduct**: corporate guidelines issued as policy requirements that regulate acceptable and unacceptable business behavior. Provisions of these codes include items such as conflicts of interest, the acceptance of gifts, entertainment and travel, proprietary information, misuse of corporate assets, compliance with laws and regulations, personal conduct on the job, reporting violations, and disciplinary actions for violations of the code.

**Conflict of Interest**: occurs when an employee or manager places his or her own interests, usually of a financial nature, above those of the organization in such a way that he or she has "divided loyalties" or cannot exercise objectivity in business decision-making.

**Employee Rights**: those entitlements which employees within an organization can claim as necessary and fundamental to their employment as persons of value who contribute through their labor to the achievement of that organization's objectives. Employee rights may have either legal or moral status, but in either case, management has an obligation to respect these entitlements, which normally include the rights to fair and equal consideration, nondiscrimination, privacy and confidentiality, freedom of speech, due process, safety and freedom from workplace hazards, freedom of association off the job, and to know of organizational decisions which may affect them.

**Ethics Audit**: a review of the ethically sensitive areas within an organization which would occasionally make recommendations for change of processes, strategies, or standards as needed; a review of an organization's past social performance in areas such as charitable giving, hiring/promotion of minorities and women, and the social impact of its internal decisions.

**Moral Maze**: ethical dilemmas, quandaries and problems encountered in the course of one's career requiring a hard managerial choice between equally acceptable courses or the lesser of a set of evils.

## Flow Diagram for Value-Based Decisions

**GATHERING DATA**
Gather all the data surrounding the decision

**IS THE DECISION APPROPRIATE**
*Base your answer according to 3 ethical standards:*
1. **Utility**: Does it optimize the requirements of all stakeholders?
2. **Rights**: Does it respect the rights of the individuals involved?
3. **Justice**: Is it consistent with the canons of justice?

**NO on all criteria**

**NO on 1 or 2 criteria**

**YES on all criteria**

**ANALYSIS**

**Are there any "overwhelming" factors?**
- Is one criteria more important?
- Any incapacitating factors?
- Pass "double-effect" test?

**NO**          **YES**

**JUDGEMENT**

The decision is <u>NOT</u> ethical

The decision <u>IS</u> ethical

## Making "Right" Choices

In order to create a culture of high trust where everyone communicates effectively, shares the vision, and is able to work unrestricted by bureaucracy and rules, the organization much reach the stage of empowered teams. When this is achieved, morale is higher, people are more productive, customers are more satisfied, and management is less stressed.

However, to really empower a team, they have to be able to make the "right" decisions. That means right for the customer, right for the employee, and right for the business. To do this, they must have the skills and a process. There are two steps to the process.

The first is developing a go/no go model for ethical decisions. After the team decides on the course of action it wants to take, it gathers all the relevant information around that decision. Who are the Stakeholders? Who has any issues? What will the issues be? After they have gathered all the facts, then they must determine if the course of action is appropriate according to the three ethical criteria:

1. **Utility**: Does the decision optimize the satisfaction of all stakeholders?

2. **Rights**: Does it respect the rights of individuals involved?

3. **Justice**: Is it consistent with the cannons of justice?

If the answer is clearly "no" on all three criteria, then the team should come to a full stop. If it is clearly 'yes' on all three criteria, then the team may proceed without requiring higher approval. The tough decisions, however, are those with "no" answers on just one or two criteria, and it would be a great benefit to the organization to proceed. At this point, the team will have to do a more in-depth analysis and explore questions such as the following:

1. Are there any overwhelming factors that should be considered which will weigh the decision in one direction or another?

2. Is one criterion more important than the others in this situation?

3. Are there any incapacitating factors?

Once these questions have been drilled into, the next step is to determine the risk of something going wrong. Risk is looked at from a two-dimensional axis:

1. What is the Probability of the error happening?

2. What is the Consequence if the error happens?

Steps here involve analyzing the probability of error. Is it large or is it small? Do the same for the consequence. Is it large or small? If the answer is small on both dimensions, then the team should proceed with caution. If it is large on both, the course of action should not be considered. If they fall in the median range, the team then should do a risk mitigation analysis to see what could be done to either re-duce the probability, reduce the consequence, or both. If this is achieved, then again, the team can proceed with caution with perhaps review from more senior management.

Why did I put this decision-making process in this section on culture? Because, I find that this process is what iLeaders do. Interestingly enough, many of them do not even realize this is the sub-conscious thought process they follow. So, if all managers would learn this, it will help organizations ensure there will be no violation of the culture or the strategic plan.

## RISK MITIGATION

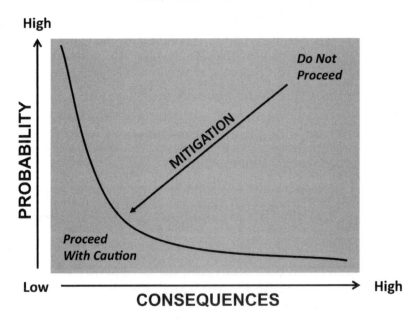

*The best way for managers to gain compliance
and motivate others is to create an atmosphere of trust.*

| VALUE | ATTRIBUTES | RANKING |
|---|---|---|
| accomplishment | completes tasks and gets results | |
| acknowledgement | to be appreciated & rewarded | |
| ambitious | hard-working, aspiring | |
| broad-minded | open-minded | |
| capable | competent | |
| challenge | active and excitement | |
| cheerful | light-hearted, joyful | |
| consistent | predictable | |
| cooperation | getting along with others | |
| courageous | stand up for beliefs | |
| creative | lateral thinker | |
| daring | risk-taker | |
| dependable | keeps word | |
| disciplined | follows orders | |
| effective | efficient | |
| expertise | being an expert in specific area | |
| fair | even-handed | |
| fastidious | fussy, detailed | |
| forgiving | willing to pardon | |
| friendship | to have valuable friends | |
| helpful | works for others' welfare | |
| honest | sincere, truthful | |
| imaginative | dreamer | |
| independent | self-reliant | |
| instructive | share information with others | |
| intimacy | share deep affection | |
| loving | tender, affectionate | |
| open | accepting | |
| organization | logical, consistent, rational | |
| pleasure | contentment, pleasure, fun | |
| polite | well mannered | |
| quality | high standards | |
| recognition | awards, status, well-known | |
| responsible | reliable | |
| security | protection, safety | |
| spiritual | inner peace | |
| self-controlled | restrained | |
| tranquil | peace, quiet, no conflict | |
| variety | enjoys new experiences | |
| wealth | financial independence | |

## Values Exercise

*Refer to the values list on the previous page and rank the top five in the order you believe represents your most strongly held personal beliefs.*

1. _____

2. _____

3. _____

4. _____

5. _____


*What do you do on a day-to-day basis that demonstrates to others that you actually live by those values?*

_____

_____

_____


*Now take the same list and rank the top five in the order you believe are most encouraged by your organization:*

1. _____

2. _____

3. _____

4. _____

5. _____

*How have you seen these values demonstrated in your organization during the past 12 months?*

_____

_____

_____

*Do any values appear on both lists? Was there any on one list that conflicted with those on the other list? Can the differences be resolved?*

_____

_____

_____

_____

_____

_____

_____

_____

_____

_____

_____

_____

_____

## Refining the Culture

In my work, I discover that many senior managers are not in touch with what employees believe to be the true operating culture of the organization. To help bridge that gap, I use a survey instrument developed by Human Synergistics® called the Organizational Culture Inventory® (OCI®).

This was designed for managers to accurately assess the culture of their organization. It provides a clear picture of the norms and expectations as perceived by everyone in the organization. The OCI™ is a quantitative instrument that measures 12 sets of norms associated with three general types of organizational cultures: Constructive, Passive/Defensive, and Aggressive/Defensive.

There are two parts to the survey. First the senior management completes the OCI™ Ideal survey. This gives them an assessment of what they believe is the ideal or desired culture required for this organization to succeed in their particular industry, as well as the culture that will attract and retain the most desired employees.

An appropriate percentage of employees then complete the OCI™ Actual. This instrument assesses what the majority of the employees feel is the actual culture. It provides feedback on how employees are expected to deal with each other, rather than with people outside the organization. It represents the behaviors that people are being consistently rewarded for and those that will result in negative consequences.

From these surveys, we are able to generate profiles and graphs that provide an accurate snapshot of where the organization is and what it has to do, specifically, in order to remain successful going forward.

The objective for doing this is to reduce the gaps between an organization's current culture and what its ideal should be. This results in an assessment against the 12 sets of norms that describe the thinking and behavioral styles that might implicitly or explicitly be required for people to "fit in" and "meet expectations" in an organization. These behavioral norms specify the way all members of an organization, or those in similar positions and locations, are expected to approach their work and interact with one another.

The norms are defined by two underlying dimensions: the first being the extent to which there is a concern for people in the organization, and the other being a concern for task. The second dimension distinguishes between expectations for behaviors directed towards fulfilling higher order satisfaction needs and those directed toward protecting and maintaining lower-order satisfaction needs.

## The OCI™ Circumplex

An organization's scores are plotted on a circular graph known as a Circumplex. Ideal profiles usually have high scores in the Constructive categories, moderate to low scores in the Aggressive categories, and low scores in the Passive categories. Once in a while, the Passive and Aggressive ideal norms are reversed for public sector organizations, with lower scores desired in the Aggressive categories.

However, quite often what the employees indicate as the actual culture is a more dysfunctional Circumplex. This is where the Constructive styles are proportionally lower than both the Passive and Aggressive styles. A summary of the styles follows each diagram.

# Constructive Cultures

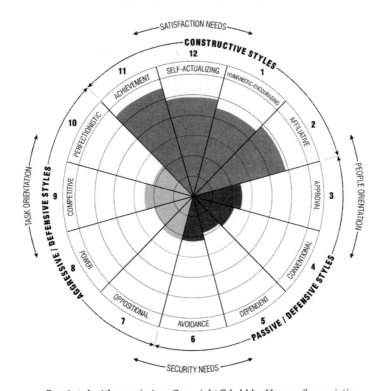

*Reprinted with permission. Copyright© held by Human Synergistics.*

**Achievement:** Members are expected to set challenging but realistic goals, establish plans to reach those goals, and pursue them with enthusiasm.

**Self-Actualizing:** Members are expected to enjoy their work, develop themselves, and take on new and interesting tasks.

**Humanistic:** Members are expected to be supportive, constructive, and open to influence in dealing with one another.

**Affiliative:** Members are expected to be friendly, cooperative, and sensitive to the satisfaction of their work group.

# Passive/Defensive Cultures

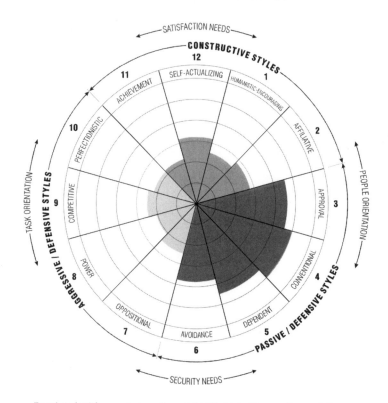

*Reprinted with permission. Copyright© held by Human Synergistics.*

**Approval:** Employees are expected to agree with, gain the approval of, and be liked by others.

**Conventional:** Employees are expected to conform, follow the rules, and make a good impression.

**Dependent:** Employees are expected to do what they are told and clear all decisions with management.

**Avoidance:** Employees are expected to shift responsibilities to others and avoid any possibility of being blamed for a problem.

Government bureaucracies commonly have a more passive culture. However, in the long term, you still want stronger weighting in the constructive areas.

## Aggressive/Defensive Cultures

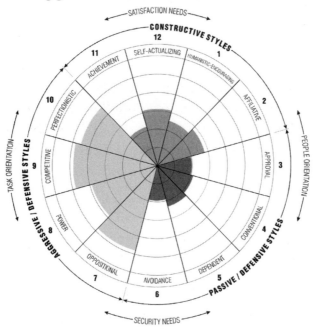

*Reprinted with permission. Copyright© held by Human Synergistics.*

**Oppositional:** Employees are expected to be critical, oppose the ideas of others, and make safe, low-risk decisions.

**Power:** Employees are expected to take charge and control others but do what they are told by managers.

**Competitive:** Employees are expected to operate in a "win-lose" framework, outperform others, and work against (rather than with) their peers.

**Perfectionistic:** Employees are expected to appear competent, keep track of everything, and work long hours to attain narrowly defined objectives.

Although this culture has been shown to produce results and be successful in the short term, in the longer term, it results in excessive risk taking, a less harmonious workplace, and higher stress levels for managers and employees. It often strains relations with suppliers and competitors.

*Business leaders today must see that the need for ethics in their organizations is greater than ever before, because social relations, working infrastructures, and technological advancements are more complex and demanding than at any other time in history.*

What I have found is that the creation of values, vision, and mission will have only marginal effect on the culture of an organization if there is not an absolute determination for implementation by senior management and a complete buy-in and commitment by employees. Senior management must also put in place an appropriate reinforcement process when they see employees making decisions that reinforce the desired culture. This behavior must begin at the top with executives being the role models for the culture.

In addition, the organization's values must be aligned with its vision and mission. If not, there will be a cultural disconnect which will result in a loss of psychic energy within the organization. People must feel a sense of pride with the organization they work for. This pride results in energy, motivation, and a sense of connection to all members of the organization.

Many times, the norms that emerge from conducting an OCI™ in an organization do not reflect the statements in the vision and mission. This is because the norms are derived from the reality of what employees face on a day-to-day basis. I have found that this disconnect will cause role confusion, personal stress, more absenteeism, and a higher turnover.

Just as a person will be remembered for the values by which they live, an organization will develop a reputation and a culture based on the choices it makes.

*The most important choices organizations make will always be balanced between people and profit.*

## How Constructive is Your Culture?

*The first step to improving any environment is to determine how constructive the organization's culture is currently. You need to have a measurement of the culture before you can develop a strategy on what to improve and how. After reading each question, rate your organization's culture on a score of one to five. When you finish, add up your score and review the results.*

| Never | | Sometimes | | Always |
|:---:|:---:|:---:|:---:|:---:|
| **1** | **2** | **3** | **4** | **5** |

1. At work, do you have the opportunity to do what you do best and enjoy?  _____

2. Do you have the resources necessary to meet expectations?  _____

3. Do you know what is expected of you at work?  _____

4. Does the environment allow you the freedom to do your best work?  _____

5. Does your manager take a genuine interest in your career development?  _____

6. Are your organization's values, mission and strategic objectives articulated clearly?  _____

7. Are your personal goals and values being met in your workplace?  _____

8. Does management value your opinions and suggestions?  _____

9. In the last six months, has your manager talked to you about your progress?  _____

10. In the last month, have you received recognition or praise for doing good work?  _____

11. Does your environment encourage and support learning opportunities?  _____

12. Does your environment support a balance between work and personal life?  _____

**Total Points**  _____

## Results

**40 or above:** Good News! You have a constructive culture. You can be a catalyst to maintain and improve the work environment. You will also improve your own emotional and physical health within this type of culture.

**Below 40:** Review your current culture and determine how you can influence the development of a more constructive environment. Take every opportunity to suggest or contribute new ways to promote an ideal culture.

**Add your own:** There may be other positive aspects of your culture that these questions did not cover, yet are contributing to a constructive environment. Feel free to list these factors below. Score these factors and add the points to your results.

## PERSONAL NOTES

*Additional factors that contribute to a constructive workplace:*

1. _____

2. _____

3. _____

4. _____

5. _____

Creating a supportive workplace culture is the first step to creating proactive attitudes. To develop your employees' attitudes further, you need to provide them with the opportunity to assess their feelings, beliefs, and behaviors.

All transformation begins by looking first at ourselves. A guide that I have used comes from an unattributed poem I heard as a teenager many years ago. I find it is still the best rudder for my decisions.

## The Man in the Mirror

*When you get what you want in your struggle for self,*
*And the world makes you king for a day,*
*Just go to the mirror and look at yourself,*
*And see what the man has to say.*

*For it isn't your father or brother or wife*
*Whose judgment upon you must pass;*
*The fellow whose verdict counts most in your life,*
*Is the man staring back from the glass.*

*Some people may think you're a straight-shooting chum,*
*And call you a wonderful guy,*
*But the man in the glass says you're only a bum,*
*If you can't look him straight in the eye.*

*He's the fellow to please, never mind all the rest,*
*For he's with you clear to the end,*
*And you have passed your most difficult test,*
*If the man in the glass is your friend.*

*You may fool the whole world down the pathway of years,*
*And get pats on your back as you pass,*
*But your only reward will be heartaches and tears,*
*If you cheated the man in the glass.*

- Unknown

# iLeader Profile

## *Danny Murphy*

*Danny Murphy is the proprietor of D.P. Murphy Inc. His company is the recipient of the Outstanding Business Community Award for the province of Prince Edward Island, Canada, in the category of Workplace Excellence. D.P. Murphy Inc., through its innovative human resource practices, provides employees with a positive, healthy and productive workplace. Through its commitment to staff development, work/life balance, fair employment practices, and employee communications, the organization provides an exceptional work environment resulting in high employee satisfaction and retention.*

Initially, Danny was an unlikely candidate for success in business. He came from a large and humble family. In college, he went into the arts and earned a psychology degree. However, most of his work experience was in restaurants, which he usually ended up managing. In addition, at a very young age, he and his brothers displayed a high degree of entrepreneurialism and an intrinsic ability to make strategic decisions that result in positive future outcomes.

Right from the beginning, his personal motivation had nothing to do with money. It was just important for him to be his own boss and be in control of his own success and future.

Danny was often criticized for some of the decisions he made, but he was independent and self-actualized. He was willing to do whatever it took to be successful and made the personal sacrifices necessary to make that happen.

During my discussions with Danny, I was reminded often of research that I had done years earlier that shows people who tend to use the phrase "Not my job" will *never* be rich. It is the people who are willing to do whatever needs to be done, and then do it, who will achieve their dreams in life. I could list many examples, one being Bill Gates, who turned down high-paying jobs with large corporations and lots of benefits to end up working in his grandmother's garage. But, as you know, he went on to become one of the richest men in the world.

One of my favorite quotes is, "Dreams are much more important that knowledge. Knowledge is limited. Dreams can take you to the ends of the universe." Danny combines his dreams with knowledge, and passion. Then takes action.

People who influenced his success and his approach to business were Wendell Barbour, Peter Paten, and Bernie Dale. They saw something in him that, at the time, he did not even see in himself. This is another pattern I have noticed in people who have achieved great success. Others recognized their strengths before they did themselves. Maybe we all should have listened to those teachers who wrote on our report cards, "Not working up to your potential."

Danny has a very optimistic (and realistic) opinion of younger people. He feels that many business people underestimate and undervalue the contribution that new and fresh thinking can bring to an existing organization. He has never limited his thinking to old, conditioned paradigms of the past. He spends most of his time with the younger generations, not only learning from them, but understanding their thinking. This enables him to understand future trends and workplace directions.

If there were anything he would do differently it would be to take even more risks and explore even more of the opportunities that were presented to him. Having said that, however, he states that he does not waste any brain space or emotion lamenting mistakes of the past, and continually thinks of how the future can be even better. This highlights his greatest strength.

He is a master at recognizing opportunities, taking risks, and building businesses from nothing into great and successful enterprises. To actually implement processes and run the operations, he hires great talented people who provide the execution and detail to develop the tactics necessary to harness the collective potential of all the staff. He believes doing this is ultimately the key to long-term success.

Danny feels that, contrary to popular thinking, the newer generations are more ethical and socially responsible, and understand the benefit of working in a collaborative culture. Therefore, he focuses on creating that culture which will attract and retain the best and the brightest. Although he feels that equitable compensation and benefits programs are important, that is just a baseline. He feels that high-potential young people are smart enough to see beyond that and recognize that a healthy place to work, with potential for growth, development, and learning, is a place where they will keep their loyalty.

He does not lose any sleep trying to reach perfection. He believes that working in a constant state of improving is more of a reality and he only wants to work with people who share that work ethic and mindset. Although he has not had much in the way of formal business or management training, he believes that training is absolutely necessary for the people who are running the operations on a day-to-day basis. He stated that it is important that you set people up for success. He does not agree with the "sink or swim" mentality or "baptism by fire" cultures that exist in many traditional organizations.

Although turnover in the hospitality industry is extremely high, his DP Murphy chain of enterprises enjoys one of the lowest attrition rates in the industry. He avoids people who present themselves as being negative or pessimistic. "The more you associate with positive and successful people, the more positive and successful you can be," he says.

Danny recognized very early in his business life that it was important to develop a constructive and positive culture if he wanted positive people working for him. He has a constant focus on talking about the culture and coaching people to ensure they understand how important it is. He continually thinks up new and innovative banners, slogans, and themes that deliver his message of customer service and happy, friendly staff.

Guest (customer) courtesy must be a way of life if you want to work for Danny Murphy. Before a new employee even gets to talk to a customer, they must complete significant hours of training at Danny's corporate headquarters. This helps staff not just understand the culture, but how to behave in ways that support it.

Danny's real strength is being able to see opportunities that others do not, taking small businesses and growing them to large corporations. However, he realizes how important it is to hire great people and promote the right people into management to make it happen. This enables him to give managers the freedom to run the business while he explores other opportunities.

*Danny Murphy is the winner of the prestigious Philanthropic Leadership Award and is the founder and owner of a premier hospitality and food service organization. Based out of Charlottetown, Prince Edward Island, his company operates Award-winning Tim Horton's, Wendy's, Holiday Inn Express Hotel and Suites, Super 8, Hampton Inn and Suites by Hilton, Stanhope Beach Resort & Conference Centre, the Dalvey Resort, and Oak Acres Children's Camp in various locations across Eastern Canada.*

# Summary

## *Chapter Five*

## Organizational Cultures

- *Various types of cultures.*
- *A case for corporate responsibility.*

## Value-Based Decision Making

- *Why is culture important?*
- *Developing values.*
- *Communicating the values.*
- *Values exercise.*
- *Refining values.*

## Connecting Values & Behaviors

- *Making the right choices.*
- *A flow chart for decision-making.*

## Refining the Culture

- *The OCI™ cultural analysis.*
- *Constructive, aggressive & passive cultures.*
- *A poem for decision guidance.*

# Afterword

I most firmly believe every employee has the right to work in a constructive environment and be led by effective managers who focus on their strengths. I also feel that most managers truly want to provide this environment. However, the reason it does not exist in many organizations is not because of a lack of desire, but because managers today have not, for the most part, been provided with the practical education and training that would give them the confidence and ability to behave in this manner.

My hope is that this book will be a guide for all managers to help them in their personal and professional development plans and inspire them to follow some of the basic principles that will actually make their lives easier.

I not only appreciate the many wonderful managers I have had in my life, but I am also thankful for the ones that were less than ideal. It is from them I learned the significant negative effect a manager can have on each individual, the productivity of the team, and the effectiveness of the whole organization. (And, it is not that they were bad people!)

Managers who get the best from their teams inspire a positive workplace culture. Some of the positive influences include the following.

- Fair and equal treatment of all employees
- Open and honest communication
- Clear goals and expectations
- Achievements recognized and rewarded
- Regular training
- Equal opportunities for all employees
- No bullying or intimidation from peers or superiors
- Open management style

My hope is that this book will provide an approach for looking at and changing your organization's culture. Using it, you can expose cultural assumptions and practices, and set to work aligning organizational elements with one another and with your overall strategy.

So there it is. To grow your business from $1M to $1B or to ensure your organization is sustainable for the long term you have to be knowledgeable and put into the practice the five concepts covered in this book:

### 1. Predict where the industry will be in the future.

This is called a Wayne Gretsky strategy. One of the things that made Wayne an amazing hockey player is that he never chased the puck. He predicted where it was going to end up and made sure he was there when it arrived. Ensure you know where you are in the evolution of organizational transformation.

### 2. Build the team.

Everyone has heard it many, many times. Get the right people on board. Ensure they are working together in a productive and positive manner. Remember the Quilting Bee concept.

### 3. Coach the people.

Forget the old carrot and stick performance evaluations. If you have ensured you have the right people, just provide effective, consistent, daily and weekly coaching.

### 4. Communicate effectively.

Learn to identify others' styles by noticing specific similarities and differences people exhibit. Managers must learn to identify people's styles by noticing their clothes, eyes, and hairstyles, and by the specific behaviors they exhibit. This will enable you to adapt your style of communication to increase the effectiveness of your message. You will also develop a better understanding of the normal or usual reactions that others exhibit in different situations, which will enable you to choose alternate responses and tactics.

### 5. Create a collaborative culture.

The new employees coming into the workforce today require a very different environment than employees of the past. They expect to be engaged with the management and work as partners. The Baby Boomers who are returning to the workplace need the same thing. iLeaders are proactive in shaping and reinforcing constructive, collaborative cultures.

Y ou can encourage attitude change by using the principles in this book. Remember, however, that you cannot change other people's attitudes; they need to change their own. But you, as a leader, can provide an environment and the resources to encourage self-awareness and effective behaviors.

It is now your choice to become an *iLeader*.

*Many people truly*
*want to improve their lives.*
*However, most will not make the effort*
*to improve themselves. Therefore, life*
*will not improve for most people.*

# Acknowledgments

My first and greatest thanks and appreciation goes to all clients I have worked with through Ethos Enterprises Inc. and Gateway Leadership Inc. for the past 20 years. I would also like to include the many managers and leaders who have attended my executive development programs that are offered through the Schulich School of Business at York University. I continue to learn the most from them because they enable me to fine-tune and advance the models, concepts, and theories I create.

In particular, I want to recognize those clients who agreed to be interviewed for this book. These are the people for whom I have extremely high admiration. They are business leaders who are entrepreneurs and strategic thinkers who sincerely place a high value for the people in their organizations, are sensitive, and continually strive to create constructive cultures in their organizations that are often constrained by large bureaucratic processes. Many of them started from humble beginnings and use their heart when executing their leadership responsibilities.

They include the following.

**Elaine Gutmacher** – Director of Operations at the York University Schulich School of business.

**James Malliaros** – Senior Vice President at Universal Studios Canada.

**Murray Smith** – Entrepreneur Extraordinaire. He is a master at building profitable companies. He once resurrected the Indian motorcycle brand and turned it back into being a successful company.

**Dr. Christopher Mazza** – Founder, President, and CEO of Ornge Transport Medicine.

**Pat Minicucci** – Senior Vice President at the National Bank of Canada.

**Danny Murphy** – Owner of numerous Tim Horton's, Wendy's franchises, Hilton Hampton Inns, Holiday Inn Express, and various other enterprises.

**Kevin Lewis**, who is the mainstay in building our business in the Atlantic provinces and is the Director of Gateway Leadership Inc.

**Mike Cassidy**, my partner in Prince Edward Island, who is an amazing business builder and an all-round inspiration to be in partnership with.

All of these executives have many things in common which include persistence in the face of adversity, determination, straight forwardness, an appreciation for hiring the right people, providing effective and on-going training, and trusting staff to use their talent and judgment in making critical decisions.

Next, my sincerest appreciation goes to the Human Synergistics Organization in Canada. Both **Allan Stewart** and **Colin Pearson** have been invaluable in my continued learning about interpersonal behaviors and organizational cultures. We have also had great discussions about connecting dots between individual thinking, behavioral styles, and how cultures are created in organizations.

To be able to work at a profession I love and one that allows me to use my skills best is a gift in itself. Not many achieve this distinct pleasure in life. At the same time, I feel very fortunate and thankful to have worked with some of the most wonderful, positive, and inspiring people on the planet. These wonderful people are the members of the Canadian Association of Professional Speakers (CAPS), the National Speakers Association (NSA-US), and the Global Speakers Federation (GSF). For many of these people, writing another book is as easy as brushing their teeth. To them it's just natural, so their encouragement kept me going.

A very, very, very special thanks (again) goes to **Susan Olsen** who continues to run my businesses, keep my schedule, and is always looking out for the "right" opportunities for both Gateway Leadership Inc., and Ethos Enterprises Inc. With so much going on, she is still able to keep our focus on our customers by providing consistent and invaluable solutions to their organizational development issues.

I would also like to thank:

**Kent Gustavson**, editor and publisher of Blooming Twig Books, who was able to take my smorgasbord of thoughts and writings and turn it into a real book.

**Ian Percy**, a friend and mentor for many years. He is the author of over a dozen books, including *The Profitable Power of Purpose* and *Going Deep*. Ian has a unique ability to help people believe in their infinite possibilities, to challenge them, and to stimulate courageous innovation. His wise and direct counsel is always appreciated.

**Brian Tracy**, a great friend, role model and laser-focused entrepreneur who helps me always maintain a goal-oriented attitude.

**Hossain Samar**, our computer genius who keeps the engines of technology running and provides his amazing creative design to the concepts. Hossain is gifted with both the left-brain logic skills to solve the most complex problems and the right brain creativity to provide futuristic solutions.

My step kids **Travis** and **Marina Arnold**, who show me just how amazing and ethical the next generation of workers is going to be.

My son, **Johnathon**, whose constant monitoring of the look and feel of the book, the cover, and the website design ensures continued visibility to our clients.

My daughter **Joey**, who is always so positive, proud, and encouraging of everything I do.

My daughter **Tracey**, who has established herself as a wise business builder and entrepreneur. She has provided me with many confirming insights through our regular visits and talks.

Finally, I have to single out my sweetheart, **Kristin Arnold**, who is always constructively encouraging, while at the same time keeping a realistic perspective on life and business. While assisting me with this book, she accomplished writing another book herself, *Boring to Bravo*, which is destined to be a bestseller. During this period, she was the President of the National Speakers Association in the United States, and continued to run her own business, QPC Inc. She continues to be a great inspiration and guide.

As Kristin would say, it is a rare blessing when a person can actually hit the trifecta of happiness in life; a wonderful profession you are passionate about, a beautiful and supportive spouse and family, and an amazing all round exciting life.

# About the Author

Joseph Sherren, CSP, HoF has been a speaker, trainer and executive coach for over 20 years working with organizations who want to enhance the effectiveness of their managers, increase employee morale, and improve bottom line results.

He started from a modest beginning as one of ten children on a farm in Prince Edward Island. Joe then progressed through a 25-year career with an international corporation where he held senior management positions in marketing, human resources, distribution and customer service. Joe received numerous awards for achievements in people management, project leadership, customer relations and education. He has been a featured speaker in management and marketing schools in Canada, the USA, Switzerland, Latin America and Australia.

Since 1974, he has trained thousands of executives, leaders, and professionals including, most recently: Scotiabank, UBS Wealth Management, Universal Studios, M&M Mars, Harley-Davidson, Walmart, Staples, and various government agencies and ministries.

Joe is currently on the Executive Development Faculty in the Schulich School of Business at York University in Toronto. He is a past-President of the Canadian Association of Professional Speakers, and has been inducted to the Canadian Speaking Hall of Fame. He is a committee chair in the National Speakers Association – USA and was the 2007-8 President of the international Global Speakers Federation.

Joe and his wife Kristin divide their time between their homes in Prince Edward Island and Arizona where they enjoy hobbies of music, horses and spending as much time as possible with their children and grandchildren.